Life, Lessons and Laughter

Discovered by a Mother Whose Son Has Down Syndrome

By Diane Cassity

Cassity Books
Utah

ISBN: 13:978-1477502402
          10:1477502408

Printed in the United States of America
Cover design by Candelaria Atalaya

Praise for
Life, Lessons and Laughter

"I learned, laughed and cried. This book changed my life!"
~ Karla Yuhas

"Pick up the book, read any chapter, you'll feel better – but you probably won't be able to put it down." *~ Mike Brown*

"An uplifting read that brings plenty of smiles." *~ Jane Parks*

"A great read!" *~ Yosh*

"With faith in God's love and a good sense of humor, this mother shows us how to take life's lemons and make delicious lemonade."
~ Michael B

"This is a book for everyone! Bound with touching stories of pure love, opportunities to laugh, and most importantly, moving experiences that enlighten and inspire shared as only this mother can." *~ Shellie Bryce*

"While my wife was reading the book, I would often hear a soft chuckle or a good belly laugh. After reading the book myself, I can honestly say that from the *"Preface"* to the *"About the Author"* and every chapter in between, I was captivated by [Diane's] writing."
~ Bryan Hurst

"I have had such an experience with this book! I couldn't wait until after work each night so I could read more, and I didn't want it to end. I felt the author's writing style equaled Erma Bombeck's and Dave Barry's." *~ Denise Wasuda*

"I thoroughly enjoyed reading the book. I could picture each event in every story, and could feel the same feelings she and her family were experiencing." *~ Karen Wilcox*

This book is dedicated to all those magnificent people who have Down syndrome. Their lives are a treasure. They fill our own lives with endless lessons and a much needed dose of love and laughter.

"But the Lord said unto Samuel, Look not on his countenance, or on the height of his stature...for the Lord seeth not as man seeth; for man looketh on the outward appearance, but the Lord looketh on the heart."
1 Samuel 16:7

Preface

Those who know Jared will tell you he possesses a warmth and love to which they are drawn. Some say that when they look in his eyes, they feel only love and acceptance. Still others say that he has a sweetness and a sort of brightness about him that just makes them feel good. I personally agree with them all, but then I might be a little prejudiced – I'm his mother.

The day Jared was born, my husband Lee and I were ecstatic! Our precious firstborn, our little son, had made it into the world with a healthy cry. Not too long afterward we were very bluntly informed that he had Down syndrome. We didn't know much about what Down syndrome really was, but we figured it wasn't good. We were devastated. We were frightened of the unknown. We didn't know what it would mean for us as a new little family.

But the devastation didn't last long. He was adorable. He had this tremendous spirit about him that made us feel happy, proud, and content. The initial tears dried up quickly. Raising him not only brought joy, but gifted us with significant lessons. Later on came an added bonus – humor. There has been a lot of it emitting from our humble abode over the years. For me, humor is vital. It's what helps us get through the rough spots in this worldly experience, and he happens to be a riot.

When I learned I was going to have another child, it was less than a year after Jared came into the world. The doctors *suggested* I have a procedure done called amniocenteses to see if the baby I was carrying also had Downs. That confused me. I didn't understand why I would need to know that. Jared was such a joy in our lives that if we did happen to have another child with this condition, it made absolutely no difference to us. We would be ecstatically happy either way. I emphatically informed them I did not want the procedure. Our second little boy, John, happened to be born minus the Downs.

Many years later, I was listening to a physician on a television show who revealed a very disturbing statistic: well over 90% of women who learned that their unborn child had Down syndrome selectively chose to abort these precious little souls. I was stunned! What in the world was happening? Had today's mind set of "being perfect" so infested our world that we now seem to feel a calloused sense of entitlement to a "perfect child" and therefore will not consider anything less?

I wondered, would these women feel the same if their unborn child had a cleft pallet, or a club foot, or a small yet unattractive birthmark on their little face? This is not as farfetched as you might think. After an ultrasound, a woman I know of was told that her unborn daughter had two club feet. Her physician *suggested* abortion as a viable option.

This was overwhelmingly distressing and utterly unacceptable to me – not just because of my own son's delightful and influential existence, but also because of the many people I know and love who also happen to be a little shy of perfection. I believe there isn't a child on this earth, perfect or not, who doesn't deserve the best this life has to offer, even life itself.

So the inspiration came. I had all the notes from 34 years of Jared's life at my fingertips. I had to let the world know what a blessing it has been to have him in our family. I wanted to share the precious, poignant, and sometimes humorous lessons we learned along this Jared journey. The love, laughter and fun that he brought with him must certainly be shared. The book had to be written. I pray that it will make a difference.

Table of Contents

At lunch, Jared was blessing the food when he heard a light sprinkling of rain outside the window.

He said,
"...and Father, we thank Thee for the partly moisturizing day."

1

Our Unexpected Journey

"All God's angels come to us disguised."
~ James Russell Lowell

There are times this life can be quite bizarre. A variety of hiccups seem to assault life's journey on occasion. Some of those hiccups result in experiences that are terrific, some end up in the difficult category, some are downright humorous, and some – well, some just *are*. But of the difficult ones, there are folks who would warn you that they "will make you or break you." That well worn cliché has been around since fruitcakes started attacking Christmas. But I'm going to throw you a ringer: the "break us" part of that cliché *need never happen*. No breaking. Surprised? I know this because I am a Knower (or so my grandson says). I have experience.

Let me share with you the two things that made this "no breaking" thing true for me and my family. First of all, I can personally guarantee that no matter what happens to you in this life, be it terrific, difficult, bizarre, or just so-so, there is always, *always* merit. The merit lies in the hidden lessons that are in there somewhere. Our job is to find them. Once the lessons are finally realized, we become stronger, wiser, and *improved*. It's the *improving* part of this life that is monumental because it is then that we rate the privilege of helping others as a result of our own improvements (lessons).

Secondly, I know that we need never "go it alone." Whenever things went from bad to worse along my own journey, I would first pray. For me that's standard operating procedure. But the Lord's S.O.P. isn't pulling a Charlton Heston by obliterating the difficult with a bolt of lightning and a puff of smoke. We actually need the difficult. Instead, He tends to use others — friends, family members, neighbors, complete strangers — to help us when things becomes too tough for us to handle alone. I like to think of them as sort of understudy angels here on earth. Most of the time they are oblivious to the fact they even *are* angels. These *other people* angels need no oversized bullhorn alerting them to our needs; the Lord gives a nudge and they oblige — giving us their wisdom, support, strength, or courage to face whatever the difficult is. Bless their angel hearts.

And the way to gain the extra help we need is the simplest thing of all. When we're in need, we just hit our knees and ask. He takes care of the rest. Oh — except for the fact that we actually have to *believe* this to be true. It's called *having faith*.

Thirty-four years ago my husband and I took an unintended detour during our own family journey. A special person came into our lives that changed our intended destination. That special person is Jared, who happens to be our firstborn. He came into this world with a little problem; he has Down syndrome. He will tell you that's why he is short. He's a little miffed about that because he would rather be Michael Jordan tall. But in addition to being short, having DS also means that he is mentally handicapped. That is not a bad thing. As a matter of fact, raising a child with a mental disability is a very, very unique opportunity.

From this opportunity we have learned so many significant and insightful things. And a real crowd pleaser is that many of the lessons we learned were laced with a good dose of inadvertent humor (of which I am a huge fan). Because the years possess no mercy and continue to plague me with more wrinkles, less hair, saggy skin, and a continual depletion in my memory bank, it is crucial one maintains a good sense of humor. It's a healthy thing to do. It's actually the cheapest face lift out there. Jared is continually helping me in that regard. He is delightfully, yet unintentionally hilarious.

Through this Jared Journey we have laughed, learned, and grown. I want to assure you that there were very few tears. To be honest, there was never much to shed a tear over, unless you count the tender type. He is hilarious! He is thoughtful. He is loving. He is kind. A big plus is that he always laughs at my jokes. My husband doesn't even do that. He is innocent, a little vulnerable, yet the strongest spirit I have ever known. He is my gift, my teacher, and my continuous inspiration to become a better human being. Jim Rohn said it best, "Whatever good things we build end up building us."

So, may I gift you with some extraordinary experiences and some great lessons we have learned on our journey. Hopefully the things I share will entertain you, enlighten you, might even change your way of thinking a little, make you smile, and maybe bring on a much needed chuckle.

Put your feet up, relax, get comfortable. I'm hoping it will be as entertaining to read as it was to experience.

"...and the Lord sent an angel..." 2 Chronicles 32:21

A fellow walked in the path of our car before we pulled out of a convenience store.

Jared yelled,
"Watch out for that Presbyterian!"

2
Futons and Post Diggers

"It is more fun to talk with someone who doesn't use long, difficult words, but rather short, easy words, like 'what about lunch?'"
~ Winnie the Pooh

Jared has a wonderfully crooked vernacular. (We don't think this is a byproduct of his Down syndrome, however. We're pretty sure this was inherited from his grandmother.) It has turned out to be better entertainment than an episode of *Saturday Night Live*. This unique "talent" has a couple of terrific benefits; it buffers day to day tedium, and it is free of charge.

Ironically, Jared's vocabulary bloopers occur as a direct result of one of his strengths. Jared does extremely well at verbalizing; he does so clearly and articulates well. This is very unusual for someone with Downs. On the one hand it has proven to be a huge advantage in Jared's social endeavors, but the "crooked" part enters the picture when he attempts to use clichés and big impressive words – they never quite come out right.

For example: upon downing a cold bottle of water after a hard workout at the gym, he said, "Wow, that was sure *reservating*!" (rejuvenating) Another time he was explaining how he had figured out a new weightlifting maneuver, and said, "...as I was *removering* into position..." (maneuvering). Then there was the time he had a buildup of that darned old *Atlantic acid* in his muscles. (lactic acid) The best part of this inadvertent aptitude is that you never know when it's going to hit, and it usually comes when you're in need of a little lift or a good chuckle.

I wondered why Jared leaned toward this propensity. Maybe it was because Lee and I had been employed at the university where Jared was occasionally exposed to cultured professors and scholarly administrators. Of course, he also hung around five teachers that happened to be within our family boundaries. That was probably the springboard for his mimicking impressive vernacular. While it is true that he likes the way big words sound, what he likes best is the way using them makes him feel – big dawg cool!

He really has no idea the words or clichés he is attempting to use are being massacred, which makes it endearingly sweet. Occasionally they come out so cockeyed that even tactful tittering isn't an option for the observer. One just has to let the laughter rip.

In the beginning, whenever this word faux pas happened and a chuckle would burst through the hearer's restrained lips, I was worried about his self esteem taking a hit. Interestingly enough, it never did. It still doesn't. He always ends up thinking it is just as hilarious as we do.

There were times, however, when Jared's vocabulary slip-ups needed adjustment for future usage in public. In that event I would say something like, "Whoops – there goes a *faux pas*." Then I would go on to make the needed correction.

Case in point: One day while we were riding in the car, he made one of his *faux pas*. We were talking about going out to dinner that night. I asked him to which restaurant he would like to go. His reply confused me. He said, "I love post diggers Mom, so I want to go where we can get some of those." A little puzzled, I asked, "Post diggers? I don't think I know what you mean, sweetie." He said, "You know – that favorite place we like to go that's Chinese. The one that has really good post diggers!" Understanding hit me and a deep chuckle reactively launched – he meant *pot stickers*. Before I could stop discreetly chuckling to explain, he smiled and said, "What? Did I make another *futon*?" (faux pas) I had to pull the car over.

Jared's *futons* have kept us smiling through the years, just as his Grandmother Georgia's did before him.   You'll find them interspersed between chapters. I figured everyone would enjoy a good chuckle. Rest assured that Jared would think it was cool that he could make you smile. So would Grandma Georgia.

"...he that is of a merry heart hath a continual feast."

Proverbs 15:15

I finished getting ready for church and walked out of the bedroom. Jared spotted me.

"Wow! Mom! You look reasonable!"

3

911 Derailed

"Everything is funny, as long as it is happening to someone else."
~ Will Rogers

There are lots of folks who have experienced using 911. We have had our own entertaining encounters with the three digit number. I, myself, own up to using it just once.

It was when I was single, when I was much younger, much prettier, and had not one wrinkle anywhere on my person. A midnight intruder attacked me in my small rented house. After a brutal physical battle, he finally broke free of the double-handed iron grip I had on his hair yelling, "Let me get out of here!" I dialed 911 after he fled out the back door. Apparently, the assailant was unaware of my profession as a university physical education instructor and gymnastics coach, or that I was an avid calisthenics enthusiast. Stupid guy. True story.

Jared has doubled my quota of using 911, as in twice. Unfortunately, both instances contributed to the mortification of his university-chief-of-police dad.

One must understand that if one holds a rather dignified position in the community, like Lee did for example, one feels compelled to keep one's head held high and to keep one's personal life modestly private. Most of the time this involves not screwing up. Lee did pretty well at this – our son, not so much.

One fine spring day I was headed home from work. A few

blocks away from our little piece of heaven I spotted flashing lights, a police car, a fire engine, and a lot of human activity buzzing around our neighborhood. As I got closer, I realized the action was in our driveway! My heart started pounding. A solid panic set in when I realized that Jared had been alone at the house for about 20 minutes as he routinely was before I could make it home from work. At that time he was twelve and very capable of staying home alone for short periods of time …*we thought*.

It all started that morning. Our alarm hadn't gone off – probably because I hadn't set it. Most people will not own up to that. Usually their excuse for being uncharacteristically late is, "My alarm didn't go off." The part where they forgot to set it is totally left out of the picture. However, I take full responsibility for not setting it the night before. (I was very tired. It was so late. The bedroom was really, really dark. I couldn't see it. And…) Thus, that weekday morning our humble abode was a scurry of late people frantically racing through bathrooms, halls, kitchen and bedrooms with the equivalent speed and duress of trying to find a bomb before detonation. Come to think of it, the end result did resemble an explosion: unmade beds; clothes, shoes, and dirty underwear littered the floors; every bathroom had wet towels thrown hither and thither; dirty dishes besieged counters; and a puddle of spilt milk lay dormant on the kitchen floor.

We are usually clean people. My husband will be happy that I am stating that as record. However, that morning we were total slobs. We were not only tempting fate, we would soon prove that Murphy's Law was alive and well.

Admittedly, the morning had been chaotic, but that was small potatoes next to the chaos I encountered on my return home. However, there was something quite fascinating that I learned as the result of the emergency vehicular parade storming my domicile. I learned what happens when a fire engine is called to the scene of a possible fire, even though no smoke is detected any-friggin'-where. Every nook and cranny, room and hall, closet and pantry and cupboard must be searched by guys in their fire gear in order to *clear the scene* before they head back to home base. In other words, our very private – uncharacteristically slobby – life was splayed nakedly before community fireman and city police officers, including the fire chief himself – all who knew of my husband and his career title.

I did not know about the thorough home search detail when first pulling up to the front of the house, however. After parking my car on the street (due to the fact that our driveway and front curbing were crowded with emergency vehicles) I hurried up our sloped front lawn and spotted our son. He was alive! Alive was good. He was conversing with a police officer and *The* fire chief. My heart was pounding, but at least Jared was safe and sound. When I reached the threesome, the fire chief took great pleasure in filling me in on the details of the event and reassured me that our house was now safe to enter. *(I swear I detected a smirk.)*

Our house being "safe" did relieve me somewhat. But since I was now well informed about what took place, I was consequently and excruciatingly embarrassed to find out that all those emergency-type guys had witnessed our unusually disheveled home …and probably my personal delicates. If there had been a large rock nearby, I would have gladly crawled under it.

However, what I was most relieved about was that, thank heaven above, Lee was nowhere in sight. *There are still miracles!* In fact, he was not due home for at least another couple of hours. This was a monumentally huge plus! If Lee would have pulled up during the fray, his Most-Dignified-Chief-of-Police Mortification Gage would have shot right off the chart. But fate had given me some time. Mercifully the mayhem would be done and gone by the time he made it home from work. The neighbors, who had been previously entertained by the day's fiasco, would safely be back in their houses and out of Lee's earshot. I would now have enough time to strategize how I would present *my* account of earlier events in such a way that would have him laughing and possibly even slapping his knee in amusement. But we've all heard of what happens to *the best laid plans* – they occasionally go south.

While I was chatting with Mr. Fire Chief himself, one of his younger overzealous firemen who knew of my husband's employment status, was currently phoning him as a professional courtesy. Darn his hide! This well-meaning fireman on the phone with Lee identified himself as being from the city fire department. He followed up saying, "Don't worry, Chief Cassity, everything's okay at your house."

A little stunned and totally in the dark, Lee replied, "My house?" His grip tightened knuckle white around the receiver.

"Yes. Everything's fine, sir. Not to worry."

"Fine???"

It was then that the old light bulb flicked on. Being a chief of police, Lee is fully aware of *standard procedure* during these "emergency" fire situations. He knew that "everything's fine" meant our chaotically cluttered house had been searched with a fine tooth comb. Mortification doesn't even begin to cover what he experienced once he put two and two together and figured out that his cohorts had witnessed, firsthand, that we were slobs – right down to his dirty underwear. I have no doubt that steam actually shot out of his ears. Yes, the proverbial cat was now out of the bag.

The fire? Oh – there wasn't one. If you'll remember, I mentioned it was springtime. In spring we leave a few windows open in the house to air out the long winter stuffiness. It also lets springtime smells waft in from the outer-world, like the smell of budding tulips, newly mowed grass, and occasionally the faint smell of dead branches and old leaves being burned miles and miles and miles in the distance. The detection of that very, very faint smoke smell certainly could be misconstrued to the untrained nose as an in-house fire. At least it did for Jared.

After the day's dust had settled (and Lee regained most of his composure), I made sure that for the rest of the evening Jared was at least an arm's length away from his father at all times. Lee did mention (okay – threaten) that he was going to hold an auction and sell Jared to the highest bidder.

In all seriousness, he was not really angry with Jared. Mortified, humiliated, embarrassed, and disgraced – yes, but not angry. He knew Jared was only performing a duty that Lee acknowledged was reasonably responsible and admittedly necessary. But that didn't deter Lee from wanting to hold that auction.

Jared's second 911 call resulted in yet another unsolicited humiliation directly involving his father. Yes, we had taught our son how to use 911, but unfortunately there are a lot of gray areas for a person like Jared.

One afternoon Lee and Jared were home alone. Eight year old Jared was happily engrossed in a television show downstairs. A commercial must have broken his attention to the story line, because he suddenly felt a little lonely. Just wanting to check to make sure there was another human being in the house, he hollered for his dad. No answer. Jared was unaware that Lee was taking a shower upstairs. If a guy needs to shower, he just disrobes, turns on the water, and steps into the shower confines. No need to announce this event to the entire household, or so was Lee's reasoning. (*It's a guy thing*.) Ergo – Jared started feeling a little panicky and a little deserted when his dad didn't respond. He called out again. Again, no reply. Jared headed for the phone...

Meanwhile, Lee had just stepped out of his shower long enough to grab a towel when the doorbell rang. Wrapping the towel around himself, he walked over to the window and peeked out. There, in the driveway, sat a patrol car – lights flashing. A thought came to mind that maybe something gruesome had happened to John and me. In panic mode, he raced down the stairs, dripping all the way, and opened the door to a scowling police officer standing on our front porch.

Lee happened to know of this particular officer. Most of the folks in our town were also familiar with him. He was sort of infamous – a rough, rigid, in-charge kind of guy who never took any guff from anyone, no matter who you were. Let's just say that he was not known for his affable nature.

There they stood, face to face: Officer Cranky verses a sodden and worried Lee, clad only in his towel, dripping on the tiled floor.

Officer Cranky: "Do you have an eight year-old son?"

A now confused Lee: "...Yes?"

Officer Cranky: "Is he here?"

A puzzled Lee: "Last time I checked, he was."

Officer Cranky: "Where?"

Innocent-until-proven-guilty Lee: "I think he's downstairs watching television."

Officer Cranky: "Could you get him for me?"

Now irritated Lee: "Why?"

A ticked-off Officer Cranky: "NOW!"

About that time, Jared hustled upstairs after hearing voices at the front door. The rest is history.

This experience did give us the opportunity to readdress the proper usage of 911 with Jared. However, once again, I had to convince Lee not to put Jared on the auction block.

After our three experiences with 911, I realized that with just our family alone, statistics proved that two out of three of those calls turn out to be false alarms. It is totally amazing to me how those 911 dispatchers keep their cool and remain composed and kind – mostly. Then there was that one time...

It happened to a friend's teenage daughter who also had Down syndrome. We'll call her Katie. Katie, who was a little naïve and quite innocent, needed some money for an activity at school. Her older brother had $127 safely tucked away in his bedroom. She happened to know this. So Katie casually waltzed into his room and helped herself to the entire wad. The "stealing" concept was unknown to her. She had never stolen anything in her life – as I said, naïve and innocent. All she knew was that she needed money, knew where some happened to be, so there you go.

When her brother found his stash gone, her little face came to mind. When he confronted her, she openly and whole heartedly confessed. But he was major ticked-off. He used words like "stole" and "bad" and "you are a thief." This was quite disturbing to innocent, naïve Katie. She ran upstairs in tears and called 911 to turn herself in.

She poured her heart out to the dispatcher who had answered her call. It is important to understand at this juncture that people who have Down syndrome sometimes have difficulty articulating words and tend to slur certain syllables together, making it rather difficult to understand what they are trying to say, as was Katie's case. So after about five minutes into her diatribe to the 911 dispatcher on what a bad girl she had been and how she should be arrested, the dispatcher, who had no idea she had Down syndrome, interrupted rather sarcastically saying, "Lady, are you drunk?"

I think that is the only time I've heard of a 911 dispatcher being anything but patient and kind. I guess patience can only go so far. That one episode does not diminish my fervent appreciation for those 911 dispatchers, however. They deserve our utmost respect and admiration – and maybe a bonus of $127. (I'll go check with Katie's brother.)

"A merry heart doeth good like a medicine:" *Proverbs 17:22*

Jared was trying to make a tough decision.
I asked what he was going to do.

"I don't know, Mom. I'm a hard rock
and a hard stone."

(between a rock and a hard place)

4

Copious Chicken Nuggets

"Sometimes miracles don't come easy." ~ *Jared Cassity*

I noticed something very strange about my little nine month-old Jared after coming home from running a few errands one evening. He looked pregnant. His belly was the size of a basketball. This was not normal. How could my son be a size 8 when I left home in the afternoon and a size 14 when I returned that evening? Even though he showed no signs of distress, I was alarmed.

I asked my husband, who happened to be the dad on duty during my absence, what the deal was with Jared's balloon-sized tummy. He looked at it. He said, "What about it?" I was miffed that he didn't seem a little more concerned than *what about it*. Then he followed with, "My belly would probably look like that, too, if I had downed three of those large jars of pureed baby stew."

"Three jars? THREE? Good grief! He was only supposed to have one jar!"

Lee was more than a little surprised by my alarm. He said, in his defense, that Jared still acted hungry after eating the first jar of stew, so Lee popped open another jar, then another. Jared downed them all. I guess that was a pretty good reason why the little guy's stomach looked like he had swallowed Nebraska.

Jared survived, but as time marched on we found this overeating thing was becoming a trend. This was worrisome. If we didn't find a solution quickly, he would end up weighing more than a Mac truck before his second birthday. So we did a little research and found that he wasn't a budding gluttonous Gerber connoisseur after all, he just didn't have a point of satiation. In other words, he never felt *full*. Had his stomach come with an informational tag, it would have read, "100% spandex."

Normally when a child eats, he reaches a point of feeling satisfied and puts the eating utensil down until the next ingestion session. This wasn't the case with our son. He never wanted to put down the spoon. It was a disturbing phenomenon.

Jared was our first child. We had no experience regarding child food control. Squelching a child's enthusiasm for victuals seemed like a daunting mission. There had to be a manual on this topic out there somewhere. We were eager to find a simple solution, like maybe duct tape. It seemed, however, that the only humanely rational thing to do would be to teach Jared about proper portion size. (Though the Duct tape concept was tempting.)

Even though portion size awareness was an excellent idea, the word *awareness* meant that he had to be, well... *aware*. Helping our child to always be alert as to portion size was absolutely imperative. We needed to make it clear that not paying attention to how much was on his plate would equal blowing up like the Hindenburg.

We fully understood the reason why over-fill was not in his best interest, but regrettably we learned from experience an additional reason. Whenever he didn't pay attention to portion size, or whenever he chose to overindulge in temptingly tasty cuisine, a nasty consequence always followed: Jared would end up taking residency in the bathroom suffering through a ruthless hurling session. That disadvantage proved not only detrimental to him, but caused grief for innocent bystanders, like relatives.

One of those innocent bystanders, who was totally unprepared for the event, happened to be my sister, Mike. Jared was about seven years old when he had his first sleep-over with his three cousins at his Aunt Mike and Uncle Fred's house. He was so excited for this first time event. Unfortunately, I forgot to mention the "portion awareness" detail to Mike. My bad.

For dinner that night, Mike baked one of her boys' favorite entrées, chicken nuggets. Jared and his three nephews sat at the kitchen counter delightfully grabbing the golden little morsels right off the baking tray and popping them into hungry mouths. Unfortunately, the "grabbing off the baking tray" wasn't conducive to portion size assessment. All four of the little guys were popping and chomping right from the tray with wild abandonment. Consequently, Jared's "nasty consequence" was about to crop up.

After the last bedtime story was read and the four boys had finally been tucked in for the night, Mike and Fred burrowed deep into their own covers heading for a good night's sleep.

About an hour later, Mike woke up when she heard a horrible and very loud retching sound coming from across the hall. (When Jared throws up, it can be heard in Lithuania.) She ran into the bathroom to find Jared's head in the toilet. Being the loving, attentive aunt that she is, she took immediate action by putting a cold cloth on the back of his neck, pressing her hand to his forehead, and supportively sitting by his side until the hurling finally subsided.

I'm willing to bet that most of you have experienced the after effect of upchucking; that feeling of immediate relief followed by a blessed tranquility in the abdominal vicinity. That's exactly what Jared experienced. He began shouting, "Uncle Fred! Uncle Fred! Wake up! It's a miracle! It's a miracle!

During Jared's spewing saga across the hall, a very tired Uncle Fred had been contentedly snoozing away under comfy covers. That is until he heard Jared yelling.

He groggily replied, "What...? What's a miracle?"

Jubilantly Jared proclaimed, "Uncle Fred! I'm better now!"

A still confused and sleepy Fred mumbled, "Oh, that's good Jared."

Mike wiped the sweat from Jared's face, tucked him back in bed, and headed back to her bedroom.

Not long after she entered dreamland, she was awakened a second time by the dreaded retching sound. She raced into the bathroom to see Jared once more hugging the toilet bowl. Once again she put a cold cloth on his neck, a hand to his forehead, and sat with him until the spewing subsided. Shortly afterward, a sleepy Fred again heard, "Uncle Fred! Uncle Fred! It's a miracle! It's a miracle. I'm better!"

Another drowsy reply, "That's... really... great..."

Yet again, Mike gently guided Jared back to bed, hoping that would be the final nauseous session so she could get some sleep. But there would be no full night's sleep granted to a tired Aunt Mike that evening. Not too long after the second episode, she again heard the loud retching sound. And once more she ran into the bathroom and assumed the position next to an ailing Jared.

After the third hurling session was over, Mike expected the joyful declaration to Fred. But this time it didn't come. He was exhausted. He was tired. He sighed deeply, weakly looked up at his aunt Mike with a very pale, sweat-drenched face, and uttered a rather profound statement for a seven year old. He said, "Ya know something, Aunt Mike? Sometimes miracles don't come easy."

He's right.

"Behold, O Lord; for I am in distress: my bowels are troubled; mine heart is turned within me;" Lamentations 1:20

I picked Jared up from mutual. His teacher hadn't been feeling well for quite a while.

Me: "How did your teacher feel tonight?"
Jared: "She wasn't there. She's in the hospital."
Me: "Oh my goodness! Is she okay?"
Jared: "They said she had to have one of those womanly sedusive operations."

5

Let It Be!

"Smooth Seas Do Not Make Skillful Sailors."
~ Old African proverb

It was midwinter; I was sitting in my toasty little car in front of Anytime Fitness waiting to pick up a thirty year old Jared from work. Couldn't he walk? After all, it's only a few blocks from home. I get it; you think I was being too soft on the kid. Point of clarification: the sidewalks in our little town are macabre places during wintertime.

Where we live, deer pay us routine visits. They like to snack on our bushes and trees. They especially love exotic tulip bulbs and pricy shrubs. It seems they have a gourmet–type taste. Why eat dirty old weeds, shriveled up leaves and dead grass on a mountainside when there's a smorgasbord of luxurious foliage down bellow? Unfortunately for the deer, we also happen to have roads. Roads have cars. Deer and cars do not mix. Ergo, walking on the sidewalks of our little community isn't for the faint of heart. Mangled deer carcasses litter them sometimes on a daily basis. I would hate for Jared to be walking to work and have to step over a mutilated corpse that once was Bambi.

As I said, I was in the car in front of Anytime Fitness waiting for Jared to get off work when he whipped out the door with an uncharacteristically huge smile on his face. Though he really likes his job, the trainers, his bosses, and even the gym clients, he had never looked quite that delighted when leaving work. There had to be some really good news behind that grin.

When he got inside the car he shut the door, took a deep breath, and said, "Mom! The neatest thing happened just a few minutes ago!"

My word – he wasn't just displaying your average *happy*, he was exuberantly happy. He was overflowing with happy, breathlessly happy. Usually he only gets that happy around desserts and Christmas presents.

He explained, "There was this woman that came in the gym just a few minutes ago. She wasn't a member, though. She was just looking around. The trainers weren't there, so I asked her if she needed some help. And Mom! She did! She asked me to help her!"

Normally, most of us would be delighted to answer questions or offer service when asked, but he was way beyond delighted. He was out of orbit thrilled. I considered that for a minute. During most of Jared's life people had always been helping *him*. Now it seemed the tables were turned. He could hardly contain himself. It was taking charge, showing her around and answering her questions that made him feel like a million bucks. But the total joy radiating from that kid gave me pause to reflect on what was really taking place. He felt *needed*.

I believe one of the most significant feelings in the world, especially in Jared's world, is the feeling of being needed. No doubt that dear woman could see that he had Down syndrome, or at the very least could tell he had a handicap. That insight must have spurred her on to *intentionally* ask him questions. She was one of *those* kinds of people – astute mixed with benevolent. Yes, there really are such people in the world – lots of them. I have witnessed their existence many times over. And this woman, bless her, made Jared feel so important that day.

Don't get the wrong idea. I am not an excessive optimist. During Jared's lifetime there have been instances where people have been nasty, cruel, obnoxious, and downright rude to him. But those people are always the exception rather than the rule. And here's another note of reality: the negative-type folks don't pop out of the woodwork just when Jared's around, and they're not choosing to be socially inept just because he has a mental disability; all of us, at one time or another, have met up with *those* kinds of people. It's a fact of life – none of us are exempt from coming into contact with foul folks. They come with this world: "opposition in all things" and all that.

However, I happen to know a secret in dealing with mean spirited people, or those who are just cluelessly rude. It was one of the gems a sociology professor taught us in a communications class at the university. It turned out to be one of the most enlightening, instrumental, and essential things I have ever learned.

The professor taught us this: When we come across rude or offensive *people*, or even when *things* happen to us which are unpleasant or upsetting, we have two choices, _only_ two: "take action" or "let it be." Taking action doesn't mean that we knock an offending person's block off or push them off a cliff. It must be a *positive* action. Taking positive action means doing or saying something that will influence the situation in a positive, productive way. Or, the other option, the *only* other option is to, "let it be." It doesn't mean we have to like it. It doesn't mean we should hate it. We just simply "let it be" – No whining, no complaining, no criticizing. Just let it go.

As I said before, there have been times when Jared has not always been received with open arms. Sometimes a reaction isn't blunt – it's more subtle. Like what we experienced trying to find him a job when we moved to a new town, for example. Finding a job for that kid was the equivalent of trying to find an Aborigine wearing a fedora and Gucci alligator pumps in the Florida Keys. There just wasn't one! After submitting applications and resumes to over a dozen establishments, we didn't get one bite, not one. Most employers were kind to his face, but either they honestly didn't have a position for him or weren't willing to hire someone with a mental disability. We couldn't prove the latter, but I'd bet my grandmother's wig on it.

It was difficult not to be sucked into pointing a finger or

trying to find a scapegoat. It was *really tempting*. But we knew better. Plus, I believe in the cliché "Good things come to those who wait."

Something else that eased my mind during that job finding endeavor was that I knew a kind, caring Heavenly Father loved Jared. We always solicit His help, so when nothing came available for Jared right away, well… we figured it just wasn't the right time or the right place or the right job. Patience is a virtue. I think I've heard that somewhere before. But faith is crucial! By golly, sooner or later, "good" happens.

That's the way it was with his Anytime Fitness position. Our job search for Jared continued for a year and a half with no success. Then during one of our routine early morning work-outs at the local gym, I happened to be wiping my face with one of the gym's hand towels. I looked at it and a thought occurred to me: somebody had to wash and fold those things. That was something Jared knew well: how to wash and fold. I walked over to him while he was bench pressing and shared the idea. "Would you be willing to try something like that?" His face lit up like a Christmas tree. The rest is history. But on the drive home, we had a conversation that went like this:

Me: I'm so excited to ask the gym management if they would consider hiring you to wash and fold the gym's hand towels.

Jared: Yeah! Me too, Mom!

Me: Don't get your hopes up, though. It's just an idea. It may not happen.

Jared: Don't worry. I won't.

Me: Can you believe that it was right under our noses all this time and we didn't see it until now?

Jared: Yeah! It was right under our noses, all this time!

There was a sort of poignant pause. He had this pensive look on his face. I could almost see the little mental cogs and wheels churning. I waited for him to spit out what was bothering him. It took a few minutes, but he finally said, "Mom?"

Me: Yes, honey.

Jared: Would you do me a favor?

Me: Sure.

Jared: From now on, would you look under my nose for me so I don't miss anything?

He's a keeper!

As it turned out, the gym actually did need someone to wash and fold the towels. That was a miracle in and of itself. But in addition, they said they needed someone dependable to clean the place. Jared fit the bill. He's one heck of a good cleaning guy. (Lots of in-our-house training.) He's also conscientious and dependable. Most importantly, the gym was willing to give him a chance. It's been the best job he has ever had. He takes such pride in the fact that the gym looks good solely due to his efforts. That alone is a huge motivator for him to do his best. *(Needing to be needed.)* And as I said before, the trainers and his bosses are wonderful to him, very patient and accepting. It just doesn't get better than that. Good things come!

However, good things come, and good things go. Like the time Jared was fired from the pizza place. Well, technically, it couldn't be called fired. You have to be an official employee to be fired. He was working under the umbrella of the high school job training project, so fired was not technically correct. It was more of a "He is not welcome here any longer so do not send him back" situation. It was all because he remembered what he was taught, and applied it: "take action" or "let it be." Frankly, the "action" part of that philosophy caused him a little grief.

It started when Jared came home from school one day very upset. He said, "Mom, I don't want to work at that pizza place anymore." From what he told me, the manager had a rather rank vocabulary, especially when perturbed. "Bad swearing," as he put it. We talked about it a little. As I remember, I mentioned that just because we don't *usually* swear around our house *...usually,* that doesn't mean he can't put up with it from anybody else. Frankly, he has his own bad habits – we all do. We must be just as forgiving and tolerant of others' foibles as we want others to be of ours. It's not a perfect world... blah... blah... blah. I ended by reminding him of the two-option philosophy: "take action" or "let it be."

One day, things finally came to a head when the manager let out a string of colorful expletives directed toward the dayshift employees that really burned Jared's ears. The *shouting it* part wasn't a plus either. I think Jared could have dealt with even that, until she threw out the G–word a number of times. You don't use the G–word in front of Jared. That pushed him over the edge. Using his Heavenly Father's name in such a foul way was more than he could take. He decided on the "take action" part. He told her he wanted to talk to her in her office.

It's a little tricky to know just when to suggest to someone that you feel they need to make a change. She happened to be in the middle of *irate*, which is not a particularly good time to suggest anything to anyone about anything. Unfortunately, he hadn't learned that part yet.

"She had kind of tight lips and her face was sort of red," he said. "It made me a little scared. But anyway, I asked her if it would it be okay if she didn't use the G-word anymore. Or any of those other bad words either." I would have given anything to have been a fly on the wall of that place when the roof shot off of its foundation. Hence, the dispelling of Jared from said pizza establishment. I was okay with that. As a matter of fact, I was darn proud. Good for him! I did the happy dance.

The bottom line is that having a job, any job, filled an enormous need in Jared. And it's not exclusively Jared's. All of us have a need to feel needed. But for kids like Jared, it's hugely, massively, imperatively important. It's like Christmas in July when someone asks for their advice or for their help. That special feeling just can't be matched. And then there's the cherry on top: the paycheck. Jared literally beams with paycheck in hand.

But before I leave the subject of the need-to-be-needed thing, I have learned something quite remarkable in that area. An incredible phenomenon occurs when it's used. It's magical. It's wonderful! I've been a witness to it many, many times. Sure, there are lots of good, upstanding people in this world who are always willing to jump in and lend a helping hand to people like Jared. At school it seems like he ran into a surplus of those superlative souls.

But the kids who went the extra mile, who really cared about him the very most, who stuck by Jared like burs to a golden retriever, happened to be the boys with hair down to their bulky bronze belt buckles, the ones that had skull tattoos with snakes squirming out of the eye sockets, the girls with body piercings in their tongues or eyebrows, the ones with the pink, purple and blue spiked fohawks, the kids who knew the school counselors on a first name basis – *those* kinds of kids. One minute they would be swearing a blue streak or flipping someone off, yet when they were with Jared, their personalities and attitudes did a total about face. They miraculously transformed into caring, trusting, responsible kids – kids who sincerely wanted to help – kids who knew they were needed, and *they* needed that.

Whatever their unfavorable backgrounds, whatever their insalubrious situations, or whatever their adverse circumstances happened to be, the need to be needed was paramount. It filled a huge void. Helping Jared gave them dignity, a sense of self-respect, a feeling of importance. That's what I've learned.

You can draw your own conclusions. Understanding the logic of it isn't really important. It just works. And it's a marvelous sight to behold.

> *"Let every one of us please his neighbour for his good to edification."* Romans 15:2

I was a little depressed and having a bad day.
I told my husband how I felt. Jared overheard.
While I was taking a long soak in the tub, Jared secretly
cleaned the kitchen and did all the dishes.
Afterward, he shoved this note
under my bathroom door:

Dear Mom,

When I heard you talking to Dad this morning about everything with the day, I really thought that I wanted to do something for you. I just want to say
I love you alot
and
you'r important to me.

Love Jared.

6

Bag the Bagger

"We don't see things as they are. We see them as we are."
~ Anais Nin

In defense of the average employer, not many of them have experience in working with those who have a mentally disability. So far, I know of no universal course called *Understanding the Mentally Challenged Employee* that is requisite for businesses. Some employers may have had experience with previous employees, so they have an idea. Other employers might have a family member with a handicap, so they have a good background from which to draw. Then there are those who just inherently know. It came with being born. But the majority of employers are unskilled, untrained, and usually fly by the seat of their pants when faced with an employee who has a mental disability.

But as parents, we were no different! When Jared was born, Lee and I were clueless. It took lots of studying, researching, plus a great deal of trial and error to understand things. So how could we expect the average employer to magically know everything we had read and experienced? Especially some of the things we learned that were very unique to Jared. Something needed to be done.

I committed to creating a condensed one page guide that would be helpful to prospective employers. It was a no brainer that by helping them it would most assuredly be helping Jared. Win–win. It also served as a handy document to have on hand for not only Jared's employers, but for extended family, friends, neighbors, scoutmasters, primary teachers and anyone else who might be working closely with him.

I've mentioned before that things have not always been hunky-dory in the employment department of Jared's life. There have been issues (sometimes several issues) that needed addressing. But as long as Lee and I were in communication with employers and they knew we were willing to do whatever it took to help Jared function well in their environment, they were willing to give it their all ...until Dewey.

When Jared began working at Marty's Market (as it will be known here) I gave a copy of the Jared Guide to Dewey (as he will be known here) who was Jared's immediate supervisor. Evidently, Dewey was not very interested in the Jared Guide. He must have filed it away under "Things to read at a much later date" and forgot about it. I'm giving him an 'F' for effort.

At the Market, Jared was a proud bagger. Besides bagging groceries, he was also asked to do a potpourri of less important tasks on occasion. But an additional task that was more in the monumental realm was what they termed "put backs." "Put backs" are those items that either the customer decided they didn't want at the check-out counter, or an item not needed by a shopper which he/she arbitrarily stuffed on another shelf in another aisle. Those items were collectively tossed in a shopping cart until it resembled the height of Mt. Vesuvius. At that point it was deemed time to do the "put backs." It was a daunting task for Jared and definitely not one of his favorites. That job took a lot of thinking, separating and organizing, coupled with time and effort.

One day Jared was dutifully doing "put backs" when he could finally see the bottom of the grocery cart. However, one of the last items puzzled him. It was a bottled drink of some sort that he had never seen in the store before. He had no idea where this drink should go. He checked the "drinks" aisle. Couldn't find it. He checked the cooler section. Not there. He looked through all the pop in the pop aisle. No match. He was at a loss. He was tired. He was frustrated. He was thirsty. There's a drink. Two plus two.

There you go. Unfortunately, the thought of paying for it never registered. There's a drink. It has no home. He was thirsty. The end.

I received a phone call at work. It was from Dewey. Not a good sign, calling me at work. Though he sounded very official, a hint of unsteadiness betrayed his practiced formality. It sounded like he needed a tranquilizer. Something was afoot.

The announcement shot right out of his mouth that my son had "stolen" something from the store. Whoa. That was a shocker. Stealing was very unlike Jared. Dewey said this was a very serious offense, and he was debating between calling the police and simply firing him. He said he was considering doing both.

I think my jaw hit the floor. It took me a minute to gather my wits so I could respond. I was certain that Jared would never ever steal anything with intent. With the severity of the situation, according to Dewey's voice, I had a picture in my head of Jared sneaking out of the market with a ten pound ham under his jacket, or the company safe strapped to his back. I began asking questions, like what it was he stole. Dewey replied, "A bottle of pop." *A what?* He told me Jared drank a bottle of pop, and he hadn't paid for it. *Was he nuts?* Wouldn't something like that require a slap on the wrist and a mild lecture? To my mind, it certainly wasn't a police-calling infraction. But the more Dewey talked, the more his voice wavered, and the more vitriolic he became. It was obvious there was more to the story. So I started asking questions.

After all the facts were in, I was a little dumbfounded. Making a mountain out of a molehill came to mind, but I wasn't going to blurt that out. (*I certainly wanted to – but again, I've learned over the years.*) I could tell from the inflection in his voice that there was still something else looming beneath the surface. Judging from Jared's past experience at the market, Dewey must not have read the Jared Guide. Darn his hide! I had the sense that he probably had a hard time dealing with Jared and his handicap, and this situation presented the perfect opportunity to get rid of some stress – i.e. Jared.

I didn't lose it. I didn't yell. I didn't do any finger pointing.

(Wanted to, but didn't) I felt I needed to keep talking with him as calmly as possible with the intent of settling him down a notch. It worked. He cooled enough that his voice almost became normal. He finally backed off the threat of canning and arresting Jared, but he floored me next when he asked my opinion of what *I* thought he should do. It was quite a transformation from the initial part of the phone conversation. It was tempting, but I didn't take the bait. It was not my place to intervene in that decision. I did request one thing of him, however: that he confer with the owner of the market and that they, together, make a decision. *That* was comfortable territory!

I didn't personally know the owner, but I knew of him. He had a reputation of being a very kind man, one who cared about his employees. Jared knew him well. Jared liked him. (Now *that's* a couple of points for our team!) There was no question that this guy would have a better solution to the circumstances than good ol' Dewey. Before Dewey hung up, he agreed that before taking any action, he would discuss the situation with his boss.

Jared wasn't fired. He wasn't arrested. The cops weren't called. No handcuffs were applied. They shook a finger at him with an added directive that in the future, he was to pay for things he used or consumed from the store. All ended well.

An interesting thing happened after the incident. Dewey showed a change of heart. Part of it might have been that I tried to be extra friendly to him after that incident. I didn't want to be perceived as a threat. That probably helped. Or maybe he finally read the darn Guide. Or maybe he just saw Jared for who is really was – a sweet, amicable kid who was trying to do his best and maybe needed a little help occasionally. At any rate, he ended up being more tolerant where Jared was concerned. He even turned into what you could call a reasonable adult friend. I am grateful for that because Jared ended up working there a number of years, and then we moved.

There were significant lessons to be learned from that experience. First, calm beats flustered every time. But more importantly, taking a positive approach by talking to Dewey in a positive way, greatly improved the outcome. It was a better alternative that throwing him off a cliff. Lesson learned!

Prior to all of this, and before getting a job at Marty's Market, Jared had been working at a renowned sandwich shop. The female manager there had been a much more patient and more understanding supervisor. He really liked her. She never wrote up an incident report after Jared artfully arranged the phrase "I love you Joan" in sliced tomatoes. She must have read the Guide.

"...he that refraineth his lips is wise." *Proverbs 10:19*

Traditionally, after a bride tosses her bridal bouquet to her bridesmaids, she tosses her wedding garter to the ushers.

At John's wedding, his new wife, Kristy, threw her garter and Jared happened to catch it.

Later, he jubilantly proclaimed, "I'm so lucky that I actually caught Kristy's girdle!"

7

Nix the Fish – Bring on the Cocktail

*"If you want your children to keep their feet on the ground,
put some responsibility on their shoulders" ~ Abigail VanBuren*

At 30 years of age, Jared announced one day that he wanted his own pet. I guess that's sort of a typical kid's request. But we already had a family pet, as in *dog*. We have always owned a dog. It's just what we do. We're dog people. I don't think we have ever let more than a few months go by without having a furry family affiliate in-house. And not too long ago I discovered why. We needed the daily fur fix. It's a proven scientific fact that stroking animal fur calms the troubled soul. (I think Dr. Betty White said that... or was it Dr. Doris Day?) So in order to stay emotionally well balanced, it was something we had to have. I'm convinced that without our daily fur fix we'd end up a sort of terse, tense, moody group.

While it was true that Jared has always had access to Cooper (our current furry resident), he just wasn't happy with the *family* part of it. He wanted his own pet. We were reticent about accommodating him on this one.

It is important for those of you reading this to understand that my husband and I have always wanted the absolute best for our children. I believe that's the mantra of most parents. But we reserve the right not to give into to every whim. For example, we never ran out and bought one of those neat little ATVs when our sons developed a hankering to go exploring in the hills. (A walking stick, maybe.) Everyone knows that giving a kid everything his heart desires is detrimental to his well being, not to mention a parent's wallet for Pete's sake. But with this *pet* thing, I began to see merit. We could actually *kill lots of birds with a bunch of rocks,* as Jared would put it. Three big benefits jumped out at me: first, owning his own pet would mean Jared would be solely in charge of its care and welfare, a great responsibility and accountability builder; second, he could watch his money accumulate toward a goal – Economics 101. Two great educational concepts in one fell swoop.

The third benefit requires that I give you a little background. Children are Jared's number one joy. He absolutely adores children, more-so than anyone I know. As a matter of fact, one of his greatest desires is to be able to have his *own* children. Now, it's important for you to understand that though Jared wants children, he did not correlate this acquisition with the necessity of a wife nor marriage. In his mind, a female counterpart isn't necessarily crucial at this point in his thought process. He had not a clue as to how he would *get* children, nor did he care about that; he just sincerely loves them and would like to have some around. While this is a hugely naive view of having children, Lee and I are definitely *way* okay with it! For Jared, having children on this earthly sphere isn't in the cards anyway. He physically is unable to procreate, which is as it should be, in our opinion.

Because we happen to be Mormons (members of the Church of Jesus Christ of Latter-day Saints), he knows that people who live righteously here on earth will have the opportunity to have children in heaven. That is a huge reassurance for him – right now though, it doesn't fill the gap. So the thought hit me: if he owns his own pet, I think from *his* viewpoint it might rank right up there with having his own child. After all, a pet is a living, breathing thing of which he will have sole custody. By darn, it might actually do the trick. There it is – he can become Dad to his pet.

What a terrific deal – three significant benefits out of one critter acquisition! We are definitely geniuses!

However, the second benefit (the money issue) would be quite the challenge. Jared understood the basic principle that earning money equaled the ability to buy things, but *amount* eluded him.

Then there were banks. Now they were a total conundrum! Even though he has heard the phrase, "The money's in the bank," if you can't see money, how can you have it? He didn't get it. Money only made sense to him if he had cash in his hand, could touch it, look at it, and count it. This whole pet-getting experience needed to make sense to Jared in the way that he viewed money.

The irony of the situation was that Jared actually had enough money in savings to pay for any pet he wanted at any time he wanted. Sure, he could draw money out of the bank, but that would prove meaningless. It would be putting the cart way before the horse. More importantly, we would be letting him down as responsible, caring parents. Isn't it written somewhere that as parents it is a requirement to make things as difficult and complex as possible for our children? I think it's a law or something.

I was drawing a blank on exactly how this pet-getting process should be done that would *kill all those birds with all those rocks*. But then I am a woman of the twentieth century, am I not? And as such I possess a colossal collection of catalogs with which the entire consumer population would be covetous. Anything can be solved using a catalog! Wasting no time, I headed straight to my mammoth mound of catalogs. I knew there would be an idea in there somewhere. If not, I could always order something to make myself feel better.

After only a few minutes of page flipping, there it was: *The Money Jar*. Bells and whistles went off inside my head. (See? Catalogs are amazing!) It was a beauty. It had a transparent plastic base with a battery powered LCD readout on the lid. The thing actually displayed a total of its contents after each coin was pushed through the slot. Technology is a wondrous thing! Jared would be able to physically handle the money, see it accumulate, and view the total amount at any given time from the display on the lid. And the price was right – cheap! Perfect! We ordered it. It came within the week. Jared proudly placed this marvelous gadget on the top center of his dresser.

The amount needed wasn't an issue… yet. What was important, we felt, was to begin the process of saving toward a goal. It was such a kick at the end of each day to watch our eager son insert the leftover change from his daily allowance into his amazing money jar. He would even try to conserve his daily spending just so he would have more coins to insert into the slot each evening. (Hey – a bonus concept: conserving!) Then, he'd proudly announce to anyone within earshot how much money he had. Wow! It was working. I am a genius! (Catalogs!)

He was thoroughly into the saving part. But now there were two more parts that needed to be addressed: the type of pet and its asking price. As to the type, I mentioned early on that we already had a dog, and owning two dogs was not an option. Cats were out, as well as gerbils and guinea pigs (been there, done that.) So with the "exclusion" list firmly established, I asked him what remaining kind of pet he might like. He said, "fish."

Geez. Fish. I will admit that I liked to watch the little critters swimming around in those huge aquariums in doctors' offices and restaurants. I even recall having a fish (as in only one) years ago. Then I began to remember the fish bowl cleaning, scraping the slimy stuff off all the doodads at the bottom, the fish food dilemma (too much, not enough) and the nasty smell that usually accompanied my little fishy resident. But it was what Jared wanted, and Lee and I were willing to make the sacrifice. So with the pet goal selected – *fish* – we found out how much a small fish tank would cost, added in the cost of a few fish, came up with an amount, and Jared was set.

Time went on, and as Jared neared the sum needed to buy the fish, unsettling thoughts of having fish in our home under Jared's care started to plague me. Fish are smelly. Fish get ICK. Fish don't do tricks for food. Fish don't communicate (though I think they gurgle a little). I even began having nightmares about them: the entire tank of fish all floating belly-side up; a giant fish leaping out of the tank and attacking our dog; the fish tank crashing to the floor with the ensuing flipping fish fiasco. As a matter of fact, I don't even like to *eat* fish. Then the realization hit me: I had never given Jared any other options for pets he might want. What was I thinking? Okay – there was hope!

The following evening, I went downstairs to his in-house apartment and asked him if there might be any other critter he would like to have other than fish. (Though if he wanted fish, by golly, fish it would be!) This I asked with fingers crossed. He gave me a blank look. This was my cue. Acting fast was paramount since no thoughts seemed to be germinating. I was mentally scrambling to come up with a suggestion, *any* suggestion away from fish. What I said next just popped out, "How about a bird?" His eyes lit up, and his excitement mounted with that idea – even more so than the fish one. Hallelujah! Jared wants a bird! I can do birds!

There are so many positives to having birds as pets as compared to fish. For example, isn't the number one reason for having a pet so that you can have some sort of interaction with it? As far as I know, there is only one interaction a fish makes with a human being: when you put your face up real close to the fish tank glass, most fish will swim toward you and ...look at you. That's it. Big friggin' deal. Here is another minus concerning fish: their memory is short – even shorter than mine, as in three minutes. No wonder the little critters can't do tricks! And while it may be true that they wag their tails, it's done with selfish intent to get from point A to point B – not as in, *I'm so happy to see you.* They just sort of ogle and meander through water. I wouldn't count ogling and water-meandering as being huge pet positives.

Now a bird will sing, chirp, respond, fly to you, and sit on your finger – with no fishy smell or sliminess involved. Lots of positives. There ya go. No contest. Bring on the bird!

We had finalized the figure he might need to cover the cost of a bird. It might run around $100, we guessed.

Now, there was only one decision left to make: what *type* of bird should he get? For this, we felt we needed to do a little research. I told Jared I would call his uncle Jerry. I did this because Uncle Jerry and Aunt Elaine owned a canary. Obviously they had vast experience in the bird area. Over the phone, Jerry went on and on about how neat it was to have a canary. He advised against parakeets or parrots because they are so noisy. Good to know. Okeedoky then! Canary it is!

At long last, Jared reached his financial goal. It was time to buy the bird. He was beyond ecstatic! He could hardly wait to get to the pet store.

Just the smell of a pet store is overwhelmingly intoxicating to a person who walks through the doors with the intent of purchasing a pet. For Jared, the anticipation was nearing the giddiness stage. Thank heaven every section of the store was clearly labeled with huge signs hanging from the ceiling. I could read them even without my glasses. If we would have had to go looking for the bird department, or even have had to stop and ask a clerk, he may have exploded on the spot. Knowing the exact direction of our target, we scurried over to the clearly labeled bird section and surveyed the array of feathery critters.

There she blows! A canary! Wait a minute; there were actually two canaries on display: a traditional yellow one and an exotically bright red one. What exquisite little birds! Even amid the pet store cacophony, the delicate songs of those two little birds flowed through the air soothing the atmospheric chaos. Beautiful! I glanced at the price tag on the yellow one. GAD-ZOOKS! I was stunned! $175 for a teeny bird, one that won't even sit on your finger! No kidding! And the red one was over the top, $250! That was just the price tag for the bird alone, no cage or food included. Good grief – you could breathe too hard on the little thing after eating at El Toro's and it would end up toast (pun intended). We eat at El Toro's fairly often. There goes $250 bucks.

I did a quick reassessment, and said to Jared, "Just for fun, why don't we look at some of the other birds, too? Maybe we can find some that are a little closer to your $100 goal." He was agreeable to that. Bless him.

After a few minutes, Jared spotted a cage full of beautiful birds. He said, "Mom! Come over here! Look at these *cock-tail birds*!" (I glanced at the sign he had just read, "*Cock-a-tiel*." I chuckled... another *futon*.) Plus these birds were larger, looked hardier, and would actually be able to sit on a finger, unlike the exorbitantly pricey canary. And the price was right — just under $100 for the bird. At this point I was willing to kick in the rest for the cage, food, toys, cuddle bone, miniature bathtub, mirror, bird ladder, millet, bird manual, training DVD, electric toothbrush, flushable toilet, etc. All he cared about was that he had $100 and the bird was almost $100, and he liked it. A perfect match! Fish and canaries were out — *cocktails* were in. Sold!

The bird he picked out of the mass of feathery bird bodies was a pretty yellow thing with a large bright orange spot on either side of its head. We excitedly called to the nearest pet store attendant. That was a big mistake. She turned out to be the pet store bird catching rookie. I astutely knew this because the moment we announced that we wanted a bird, her face drooped a little. Not a good sign.

Jared and I stood anxiously waiting next to the large bird filled cage while the attendant fetched the store's magic bird trapping gizmo. I knew my initial assessment of her inexperience was right on the money when she missed her target on the first thrust resulting in the bird's escape to store freedom. It took a lengthy period of scrambling, spinning, sweating, wheezing, and chasing before she was able to retrieve our little yellow escape artist.

Now at the check-out counter holding Jared's new winded and ruffled pet acquisition in its little transitional pet box, I asked Jared what he was going to name it. He thought about it for a minute and then announced, "Sunny!" I thought that was way cute for such a bright, pretty yellow bird. However, later on that day, after we had set up the cage and all the bird toys, food, and paraphernalia, he explained his reason for choosing the name. He was so excited to own a living, breathing thing — it was just like having his own *son*.

You guessed it. It wasn't *Sunny* after all, it was *Sonny*. He finally got the kid he has always wanted. An added bonus was that this bird was supposed to live to a ripe old age of 25 years — it said so right in the *cocktail* book. It looked like Jared was set for the rest of our natural lives.

By the way, as things usually go, what started out to be a $100 venture ended up *way* over the top. Evidently the excitement over the purchase of the bird blocked Jared's reasoning, because he never cared about adding up the final numbers. Hence, he was unaware of the total expense. Neither was my husband. Had he ever done the math, he would have confiscated my checkbook and forced me to do Jared's computer math drills.

Here's a side note: as it turned out, the perky little feathery guy was not a finger sitter. I gave it a good college try a couple of times. Evidently, he's agoraphobic. I've got the scars to prove it. His condition was probably a direct result of that rookie store clerk's attempt at bird catching which left him mentally and emotionally traumatized. How sad is that? It had to be the reason behind his morphing into a miniature Cujo whenever I tried to coax him into leaving his cage confines. Whatever the case – Pretty Little Yellow Traumatized Bird will continue to remain in his rather large and well equipped cage until hell freezes over.

This leads me to something astonishing I later found. After repeatedly trying to teach Sonny to talk, I checked the manual again and found, in fine print, that male cockatiels talk, females usually do not – instead, they tend to hiss. Dead giveaway. *He* wasn't a *he*. *He* was a *she!* So here's what I think. Not only did I have gender wrong, I don't believe Sonny had agoraphobia after all. I think he has PMS.

"...the prudent are crowned with knowledge." Proverbs 14:18

Jared was impressed watching his brother John
and John's friend, Ty, move our piano.

"Wow, John! I'm just glad I'm not
half the man you are!"

8

Halloween Shenanigans

"Every survival kit should include a sense of humor."
~ *Anonymous*

When John and Jared were three and four years old, respectively, they were a little too young to understand the whole Halloween thing. Now that I think about it, I've been a little confused over the concept of Halloween myself. It *is* a rather odd holiday.

I remember trying to finish washing a recurrent mound of dishes one October day when the kids were very bored. I had a three year old kid tugging on my pant leg and the four year old pulling on the back of my shirt, both droning, "Maw-umm, Maw-umm." I knew that if I got their attention focused on something else for just a couple of minutes, I could finish the last few dishes, so I put on my perky face and asked, "Hey, do you guys know what holiday is coming up?" They stopped tugging on my shirt and pants long enough to give me a blank look. *Holiday* didn't seem resonate. "You remember that spooky holiday when you get to go trick-or-treating?" I could see a glimmer of recollection. At least they had stopped tugging and whining. "So," said I, "what do you want to be for Halloween this year?" They still looked a little confused. "Remember? Everyone dresses up in costumes, like a cat, or a dragon, or a pumpkin." They were starting to remember. "So what do you guys want to *be* for Halloween?"

You could see the wheels turning in John's little head. It only took him a couple of seconds to decide. He looked up at me and with conviction said, "A bulldozer!" Interesting choice. It was no surprise, though, given the fact that he loved every type of earth moving machine ever invented.

Then I asked Jared, "What do *you* want to be, sweetie?"

He didn't pause, "A hot dog."

Oh boy.

Years passed and we never did have to rig up costumes to resemble a bulldozer or a hot dog ...that is until several years later.

When Jared was 32, to say that shopping for a Halloween costume was a challenge would be an understatement. Keep in mind that Jared has a young mind in the body of an adult. He didn't want to be anything scary. He doesn't like scary. He wanted to be Captain America. Sadly, after visiting every store in our area, there were no adult costumes resembling Captain America to be found. What we did find in the adult attire were scary skeletons, chilling devils, evil jesters, and hairy monsters with blood dripping from pointy teeth. No Captain America. The hero-type costumes we did find, however, were the tongue-in-cheek type: corny looking outfits meant for laughs. From Jared's point of view, Captain America, Elton John, and Elvis Presley should not be laughed at.

The outlook was bleak. The only other alternative, it seemed, was to construct a homemade Captain America costume, and that was most certainly *not* an option for me. I was 62, sewing machineless, not clever nor inventive, certainly not able, and was somewhat tired. I needed to find something, and fast.

At the last store, I anxiously searched through the racks of costume attire. The outlook was bleak, until a rack with some rather unique costumes caught my eye; a bottle of catsup, a banana, a box of cornflakes, and a hot dog. HOT DOG! Hey Jared! He looked at the hot dog garment, and he laughed when I told him about his costume dream early in life. He smiled broadly and accepted the challenge this year to walk around as ground-up pork.

Halloween was still a couple of weeks away, and my husband was not thrilled with the hot dog choice. It was easy for him to judge. He wasn't the one trying to come up with a costume idea, or the one who would have to actually make one if we couldn't find one. Nope. The hot dog outfit would work just fine. But it wouldn't hurt to give it a trial run.

Two weeks before Halloween there was the annual Halloween party at his Aunt Mike's house which involved relatives. Relatives love you and are kind. That would be a perfect arena to test Jared's comfort level in his weenie and bun apparel.

The party is such a fun event: lots of kids; lots of great food; a pumpkin carving contest; and a visiting witch (that would be me). Witch Wanda, with exaggerated pursed lips and a large rubber lizard fastened to her shoulder, "flies" in on her frizzy broom to judge the carved pumpkins and to recite Halloween riddles and Monster Goose rhymes to the kids in her best Julia Child voice.

This witch thing began when Mike, my sister, and I realized that having a witch at an October party was essential Halloween protocol. Mike was in charge of the party, so I volunteered to do the witch gig.

The aim of Wanda's costume was to entertain, not to frighten. After all, there are always several very young children that would be in attendance. But what was most important to me was to conceal my identity. I didn't want them to know it was Great Aunty Diane under that get-up. It worked, too. The first time I looked in the mirror I shocked myself. Last year I knew I had succeeded when my brother-in-law mentioned how nice it was of *that lady* to play a witch for the party.

However, something bothered me a little about the whole thing. I got such a kick out of dressing up to disguise myself in witch's garb: why *was* that? It struck me as a bit bizarre. Was I turning a little psycho? Lots of people did it, didn't they? I finally realized that there was a deep seeded psychological explanation for going undercover: it gives a person license to talk and act weird, and no one points an accusatory finger. Other than Halloween, I'm thinking that's why so many people dress up like clowns. Scary thought!

The time was drawing nigh and Jared and I came up with a

workable plan that would get him involved in his hot dog gear at the party. When Witch Wanda started her Monster Goose rhymes and riddles, she would call for *that young man* (enter Jared) to come out and assist her with all her ghoulish props. (Keep in mind that Jared's costume did not call for make-up or a mask. His face was fully recognizable between the buns sticking out of a big hole in the front of the wiener. He said that maybe I could tell the kids Witch Wanda had used her magic to change him into Hot Dog Man. That worked for me. Then, judging from the response of the party crowd and his level of comfort in a weenie costume, he could make his mind up as to whether or not he wanted to keep the hot dog idea for the rest of Halloween. It seemed to be a perfect plan.

The night of the party, Wanda's entrance turned out to be less than ideal. Like I said earlier, I initially had a perfect plan: while all the party goers were busily engaged in carving pumpkins for the contest, I would subtly slip downstairs, change into my witch's garb, use the basement stairwell to slip outside, move around the side of the house, out the gate, waltz up to the front door, ring the doorbell, and Witch Wanda would make her entrance. Voilà! Things would have gone as planned, too, had it not been for the gusty wind that night.

My costume was donned, make-up was applied, and the last item to put on were my glasses (a necessity if I wanted to actually read anything.) It turned out that those specs served a dual purpose; not only did they make it possible for me to see, they also held on my warty witch's nose.

The nose thing had been a problem years earlier. You see, sticking a fake nose on one's face isn't hard, but making it stay there is tricky. Glue doesn't cut it, especially when you're a grandma with hot flashes. Sweat melts face glue. I found that out halfway through reading Halloween stories to Jared's class back in elementary school – my witchy nose slid right off my face. I had to do some fast explaining to a circle of startled children. So this time around I experimented and found that a tightly fitting pair of specs held the witch's old schnauzola firmly in place. No glue involved. I am a genius.

Now geared up and ready for the gig, I headed for the basement door; my rather bulky black bag full of props in one hand, witchy broom in the other. I reached for the door handle pressing the lever down with my elbow, pushed it open with my shoulder, ducked my head so my tall and rather wide brimmed witch's hat wouldn't get knocked off by the door frame, and stepped into the rarely used, dark, spooky stairwell.

As I turned to walk up the stairs, I was startled by two very curious dogs warily surveying me from above. They belonged to two of my grown nephews: one pooch was a large cockapoo and the other was a substantially huge and rather beefy boxer. Neither dog knew me well, let alone in my witch's get-up. I think I've said hello to them a couple of times. Instinctively, with undertones of fear and concern, I blurted out burbling baby talk in the most melodic and nonthreatening voice possible. I wanted to make sure they knew I was friend, not foe. It seemed to be working, until my foot hit the third step.

Right then a gust of wind whipped through the stairwell giving flight to a reservoir of autumn leaves nestled at the bottom. It created a whirlwind that caught my cape and long stringy witch hair. Everything was flying and whipping and airborne. I'm struggling to keep my balance with the bulky bag in one hand, trying to keep my witch's hat from flying off my head with the other while trying not to lose my broom. The spiraling spectacle sent the dogs into a growling, barking frenzy; the kind that typically pre-empts a dog attack. I was terrified that I might lose a witchy leg or a witchy arm, or at the very least, Witchy's sticky rubber lizard, which was now totally entangled in a swirling mass of very long grey witchy wig hair.

Things were looking grim for Witchypoo. I knew I had to make it to the front door ASAP. If I didn't get away from those petrified pooches, the partygoers would hear the barking mêlée and run to check out the commotion. They would spot me in terror mode. Plus, my grand entrance would be history.

I took a deep breath and made it to the top of the steps. I didn't dare turn my back on the dogs for fear of exposing a much

51

larger and more tempting target, so I began inching backward toward the gate, maintaining eye contact at all times, the dogs not three feet from my shaky knees. The melodic babble I continued to make wasn't cutting the mustard. The wind wasn't letting up, and my cape and wig hair and dress were flying wildly. The dogs kept barking loudly and frantically. It was piercing my resolve. The situation was deteriorating. But what was Witch Wanda? A coward? A yellowbellied jellyfish? ...yes.

I took another deep breath. I straightened my shoulders, (that always seems to help), kept backing up, and finally made it to the fence. Slowly, so not to further antagonize the already frenzied pooches, I reached behind my back to unlatch the gate. Inching a step at a time, I slipped through the narrow opening, trying to keep the dogs safely corralled in the backyard.

I made it! I latched the gate. Victory! Until I backed into an overgrown rosebush. Its long thorny tentacles engulfed me; my flying cape, my swirling witchy hair, even the netting on my hat, were trapped. I was prisoner to a groping rosebush!

I began to panic, which any normal witch would do under the circumstances. It was pitch black. The gusts of frigid wind were relentless. I was outside, trapped at an isolated corner of the house, and none of the adults inside were aware of my calamitous predicament. To add to my pickle, a few icy raindrops began to pelt my face. The gusts kept repeatedly whipping every particle of clothing into the arms of the barbed bush. The dogs' incessant barking added to my angst.

I knew I had to calm down, otherwise I would start flailing. Flailing would only complicate things. So I reflected on how hilarious this incident would be one day, looking back. At the time, however, there was no laughing involved.

The wind was blustery cold, the dogs were still barking, and I was trapped by a rosebush in the dead of night instead of on a covered porch, ringing the doorbell to a nice, warm, safe house. Freedom was so close I could taste it. But everything seemed to be working against me. Just as I would painstakingly pluck one particle of clothing from the grip of the nasty barbs the wind would whip another particle into its clutches. I swear that bush was alive. I was at the mercy of a stinkin' plant!

Age and experience has taught me that losing control isn't a plus. I took a couple more deep breaths, straightened my shoulders *again,* and then cautiously, yet tenaciously, plucked away at cape material and wig hair and hat netting until I was finally free of the bristly bush. On wobbly legs I hobbled around the corner of the house and up a slight incline to the final destination: the front door. I had made it! My entrance was a little shaky, but good!

Witch Wanda had all the children's rapt attention, eyes wide with wonder as this funny looking witchy woman and her frizzy broom gave an award for each cleverly carved pumpkin.

After the pumpkin judging, Wanda Witch was ready to face the troops with her rhymes and riddles and props. That was Jared's cue to get ready to make his entrance.

Witchypoo yoo-hooed for the young man she had turned into a hot dog. Initially, my plan was for Jared to come out of the bedroom in his hot dog costume, walk over by Witch Wanda's side, and dutifully assist with her spooky props. That wasn't quite the way it went. Out *bounced* Jared – literally! He was twirling and dancing and tittering. I was stunned. That was not the norm for my son. He obviously was in theatrical party mode. I had no idea Jared possessed such a dramatic flair. He seemed to be in his realm of glory with his face poking out of this funny weenie get-up. During his striking entrance he uttered, in a sort of haltingly squeaky sing-song voice, "Look what happened to me! My *mother* turned me into a hot dog!" He pointed directly at me – with fervor. My cover was blown!

Fortunately, most of the kids didn't seem to mind that it was Great Aunty Diane in the funny get-up. The rhymes and riddles kept them entertained, along with the accompanying rats, spiders, snakes, and potions.

When it came time to read the monster poem I had written for the occasion, I was a little uneasy. To make the poem a little more fun I had brought a monster-type mask along with costume hands sporting long hairy fingers that sprouted pointy black fingernails. I had intended to ask one of the kids to volunteer to don the monster attire, but as I surveyed the group of little tykes surrounding me, I was worried that the monster mask and hands might just be a little too scary. Then an idea took form. A monster hot dog! Now *that* would be more funny than frightening. *"Jared! – on with the monster stuff!"*

Monster Hot Dog was a hoot. Picture, if you will, a giant hot dog sporting a screwy looking monster mask, swaying back and forth, wriggling long hairy fingers while I read my *"Monster 'Neath My Bed"* poem:

There's a hairy scary monster
Living 'neath my bed.
I'm pretty sure he's under there,
Though he's never showed his head.

I'm scared he'll grab a wayward foot
And gobble up my toes.
So I tuck the covers 'round me tight.
With just my nose exposed.

So far he hasn't eaten me,
Of which I am most grateful.
I know I'd make a tasty treat.
In fact, a whole darn plate full.

Maybe I should set a trap
To thwart the creepy ghoul.
Like dump a hundred marbles
Next to my bedside stool.

But wait... that might prove fatal –
To me, more so than him!
A sleepy haze might dull my wits.
Oooo! That outcome is grim!

But thanks to Mom, she saved the day!
Said, "Light brings them bad luck.
It's true," said she, "Exposed to light,
The brightness makes them upchuck!"

So now my night light shines and glows
And keeps the beast at bay.
He'll have to leave the feast of me
For another, *darker* day.

I had a tough time holding it together. Jared turned out to be a creepy but funny mustardy hit. Who would have thought?

All things considered, the evening ended well. Jared got to test drive his hot dog outfit and did not seem to feel self-conscious walking around in a bun. His dad was grateful, but was still a little miffed. (Must be a male ego thing) Wanda Witch was out of the cold and away from rabid rosebushes. And most importantly, her warty nose never did slide off her face.

I learned three things from this experience: (1) my son had a flair for the dramatic; (2), things *rarely* go as planned, and (3) keeping one's cool under extreme pressure is paramount to a good entrance. Witch Wanda was invited back the following year, but would only come on one condition: that all rose bushes around the house were trimmed and covered with metal netting.

"For after much tribulation commeth the blessings." D & C 54:4

Grandma, while watching TV one night, kept falling
                asleep in her recliner.

Grandpa: "Honey, why don't you go put on your nighty
            and go to bed?"
Grandma: (yawns) "No. I'm okay. I'm just resting
            my eyes between commercials."

9

Looks Like We're Going to Holland

"Some luck lies in not getting what you thought you wanted but getting what you have, which once you have got it you may be smart enough to see it is what you would have wanted had you known."
~ *Garrison Keillor*

There is a rather well distributed story written by Emily Perl Kingsley, one of the writers for Sesame Street. When her son, Jason, was born having Down syndrome, she felt a need to explain to her friends, relatives and neighbors how she and her husband felt about it. So, she wrote a story.

She compared having her son, Jason, to an unexpected trip to Holland. In essence, she said that having a baby with Downs was like planning an exciting trip to Italy. But unexpectedly, your plane lands in Holland instead. You argue with the stewardess saying you bought a ticket to Italy, not Holland. You've planned and saved for this trip to Italy all your life. You wanted to see the coliseum, Michelangelo's David, and the gondolas in Venice. But now you're in Holland, and there you must stay! Well, we were on our way to Holland.

❧

It was late afternoon. The small hospital room was quiet except for our pediatrician's incessant supersonic mumble – a brilliant man whose mouth seemed to be stuck in fast-forward. He talked faster than most people's brains could keep up, especially mine. Being a close friend of the family didn't seem to help. You'd think familiarity and sentiment would have triggered a compulsion to gear down. Instead, his pitch and tempo had increased. It didn't help that the small private room was very cramped due to all the chairs that had been brought in to accommodate my husband, my mother, father, mother-in-law and father-in-law. The chair backs surrounded my hospital bed, and the doctor was standing in the only available floor space by the door. It was all making me feel a little edgy and claustrophobic.

I had heard his presentation before in the recovery room, just him and me, alone. My husband and family had all gone home earlier because there had been no indication of anything amiss after the delivery of my baby. Now they had all returned to hear the doctor's news.

Back in 1977, there was no such thing as prenatal ultrasound or sonograms. If an inherited or genetic disorder was suspect, amniocentesis was performed. Amniocentesis is a procedure where a needle is inserted directly into the womb to extract amniotic fluid which contained cells shed by the fetus. The fluid is sent to the lab where a diagnosis can be made. But because there was a possible danger to the health of the baby, the procedure wasn't used unless there was some indication that something was wrong with the baby. I had no indications of anything wrong during my pregnancy, so amniocentesis wasn't even a passing thought. Being my first pregnancy, everything to date seemed normal, at least according to my gynecologist and all the books and medical material I had read.

When the delivery time had arrived, I was as ready as any woman could be for the grunting, groaning, and grueling experience of childbirth. Into the delivery room the perky little nurses wheeled my gurney, giving me confidence that the world would be a brighter place when the pushing was over.

Because this was my first delivery, I was a rookie in the realm of the birthing world. I had no idea how a brand-spanking-newborn infant ought to look up close and personal. When the nurses placed my new bundle of joy in my arms, his cute chubby round face with his oriental looking eyes and his short stubby little fingers didn't seem unusual to me. Nor was I familiar with Down syndrome, so I had no idea my new little boy possessed those telling characteristics. I was just darn happy he had a healthy cry coming into the world, that I had actually made it through labor, and that I was now reveling in the joy of new motherhood.

My husband was relieved the ordeal was over and that the little stinker made it out without a scratch, with one exception: the top right side of his head was sort of pointy. They said it happened when the suction device tried to coax him out of his former residence. Lee could live with a little lop-sided pointy head, he was just glad our baby was "healthy." I thought *I* was exhausted from the ordeal, but Lee looked worse than I felt. It didn't take much to persuade him, his parents and mine, to take time off and head home for some peace and rest. I assured them I would be fine.

In the recovery room I was alone at last. It felt a little weird since I had just experienced the most beautiful moment in my life, despite the enormous exertion. I wanted to celebrate, but I was just too tired. It was hard to believe that at twenty-nine I had finally taken on a parental role. I chuckled to myself. In my head I could hear my parents saying, "It's about time!" They would never say that out loud, but I knew it was in their thoughts.

After all, it took me until I was twenty seven years of age before I even considered marriage. I was just too happy and busy with my career at the university to worry about getting too serious with any relationship. Plus, after so many years in the dating scene, it became annoying and wearisome.

But then along came Lee. He was university police. When our paths crossed, the cop in him was an indomitable and unrelenting force. He didn't let up. We dated everyday for a week and a half and married one month later. (I swear there was no shotgun involved.)

My thoughts were interrupted when the recovery room door swung open. In walked the doc with *the troubling look*. He wasted no time informing me that there was a problem with the baby. I felt my heart skip a beat. He asked me if I was familiar with Down syndrome. I said I was not. Then he hit me with the term that, today, is totally inappropriate: "Mongoloid idiot."

I didn't know what that meant, but it sounded so horribly bad. Those words brought an immediate picture to mind of a severely retarded child, *my child*, drooling profusely, sitting on the floor banging his head against a wall. Why that particular image came to mind I have no idea, but it was devastating. The tears exploded from my eyes and I felt like an elephant had just jumped on my chest. Just moments before my entire world had been euphorically happy, now it seemed to be falling apart.

My nature, however, was not to weep and wail until my tear ducts dried up. I had my initial hard cry. That was enough. I was close to God, and I trusted Him, did I not? I knew He was fully aware of the situation. He knew exactly how I felt. And somewhere in the recesses of my mind, I remembered His words, "Lean not unto thine own understanding. In all thy ways acknowledge Him, and He shall direct thy paths." It is amazing that even thinking about God in a time of distress brings a blessed calmness to one's soul.

After a good initial cry, I was ready to face things head on. I was tough. I was a physical education teacher and gymnastics coach. I could do this. I began mentally coaching myself: I would be strong; I would handle the challenge; I would be a good mother; I would do everything necessary to help my child in every way, even if it meant doing it as a single parent.

I hate to admit that at this point I was being rather dramatic and too self-absorbed. I was thinking the foolish thought that my husband might leave me, that he might not be able to handle the circumstances. I certainly didn't give him much credit. I will always feel badly for not having had more faith in his strength, his integrity, his love and devotion.

Back in those days it was basic procedure that three to four new mothers were assigned to share one hospital room. Normally, room sharing offered new-mother roommates the opportunity to converse and celebrate their newest little family additions. At the time, I didn't feel like celebrating. I was grateful the hospital automatically changed my room assignment to private status.

The doctor called my husband and family back to the hospital. They knew the news was not good. They all solemnly converged into my private room with worried faces.

The doctor entered. His discourse sounded distant to my ears in that small, confined room – like a bee's buzzing. I had no intention of listening to what he was saying; I had heard everything he had to say earlier. I had a much more significant intent. My focus was entirely concentrated on my husband's face. I didn't want to look away or I might miss the slightest hint of an expression that would give me a clue as to how he felt; what he was thinking. I would then be prepared for whatever consequence was to come.

Lee sat stoically still, listening to every word the doctor spoke. His face looked rigid, strained. It was starting to scare me. After the doc finished his rather lengthy and very discouraging discourse, ("It will be very difficult; He will have a hard time learning; Eventually he will probably have to be institutionalized, etc.") my husband finally spoke. Without hesitation he firmly and assertively declared, "It doesn't matter. He's our son."

If I were the most masterful, scholarly English professor on the planet, I wouldn't have been able to come up with such a succinctly eloquent phrase that made my whole world break into song! Not once had I thought of those precious words that put everything into perspective; *"Our son."*

First and foremost, Jared was *our son* – a wonderfully alive little boy, *our boy*, who just happened to have a little problem. I wish I would have been physically able to jump out of that bed and throw my arms around my dear husband and kiss him until his head fell off. Yes, things were going to be *– just – fine.*

After everyone went home for the second time, I sat alone in the privacy of my special room in deep reflection laced with concern. It certainly wasn't going to be easy, but we had strong supportive families, and I was now confident that we would be able to face whatever lay ahead *together.*

A knock on the door disrupted my contemplation. In walked

a young hospital volunteer carrying a huge vase full of two dozen red roses. I had never ever received *two* dozen roses in my life. They were the most beautiful roses I had ever seen. I took the note out of the middle of the magnificent bouquet and read five short words: "Thank you for my son." I fell even more in love with my husband.

It was now very dark outside and getting late, yet I had still not seen nor held my son since giving birth. As I stared at my beautiful roses, questions began swimming through my head: how would he look; how would he feel in my arms; how would *I feel* when I saw him now that I knew he had Downs?

After what seemed like forever, the door slowly opened and a nurse peeked into my room. I'm sure she wanted to see how I was fairing before she brought my baby to me. She asked me if I wanted to hold my son. Fear mixed with trepidation mixed with uncertainty pierced my resolve, but I nodded *yes*. The moment had finally come. In walked the nurse and placed the little bundle of Jared in my arms, and left.

It was just him and me. I remember everything being so quiet. It was like the world had soaked up all of the sound. He was so warm and cuddly. I looked at his little round face. He didn't look like what I had imagined he would look like after the doctor's diatribe. He looked ...precious. He felt ...precious. He was ...beautiful! He squirmed a little in his tightly wrapped blanket. Then he opened his eyes and looked directly into mine. How can one describe love, joy, reassurance, relief and peace in one fell swoop? The spirit of my little son filled that room to overflowing! It filled *me!* I didn't think it, I *knew* it; everything was going to be fine – absolutely, wonderfully fine.

Earlier, my mother asked some interesting questions. She wondered out loud if Jared's condition was a direct result of something we had done wrong. Maybe it was because of something we hadn't done that we should have done. Were we being punished? It took a little time to figure out the answers to those questions, but we did find the answers:

And as Jesus passed by, he saw a man which was blind from his birth. And his disciples asked him, saying, Master, who did sin, this man, or his parents, that he was born blind? Jesus answered, Neither hath this man sinned, nor his parents: but that the works of God should be made manifest in him. (John 9:1-3)

Things just happen in life. Sometimes they are good, sometimes they are hard, and sometimes they just *are*. But the marvelous thing about those things we experience is that there is always something to be learned in every case. And if we learn those lessons, then we grow, and we become better and stronger and wiser. We are then able to handle other situations with more dignity and more serenity and more understanding. It's a marvelous thing, this life. And God's gift to us is allowing us to come to this earth in order to have those experiences from which we learn.

But the most important thing I've learned from all of this is that we are not alone. We do not have to experience these things on our own. We couldn't even if we wanted to. We mortals are just not equipped. Christ made a promise that his love will always be there for us. He promised there will never be a dark night that does not end, that "joy cometh in the morning." He gives us His comfort, His strength, and His companionship, _if we seek it!_ That's what gets us through! The joy did come, and it came in a magnificent chubby little package. I learned that in a private hospital room holding my infant son so many years ago.

And as Jared grew, it became apparent that he was closer to God than anyone I knew.

We didn't make it to Italy. We landed in Holland. But the point is that we weren't taken to a terrible, frightening place, full of pestilence, deprivation and disease. It was a wonderful, beautiful place. It was just a different place ...and we were ready to go sightseeing.

"I will not leave you comfortless: I will come to you." John 14:18

Jared read a sign in someone's yard that said,
"Concord grapes for sale."
Out of the blue, he said, "I don't like Concord grapes."

Keep in mind that Jared does not know a Concord grape
from a seedless, white, checkered or polka dot grape.
So I asked him why.

He said, "Well, ...they're just, ...too, ...too, ...Concordy."

10

Freddy Krueger Jr.

"Laughter and tears are both responses to frustration and exhaustion. I myself prefer to laugh, since there is less cleaning up to do afterward." ~ Kurt Vonnegut

Diving into the manly world of shaving was a real trip. We knew that when Jared reached the age of facial hair we would need to be ready to teach him the art of razor proficiency. This was a scary thought; putting a lethal weapon in the hand of our son, and then asking him to swipe it around the vicinity of his exposed face and neck.

We initially tried the less worrisome method; an electric shaver. That did not work very well. We'd often spot odd little patches of five o'clock shadow sprouting around his face about noon. He blamed this strange facial hair phenomenon on his electric shaver. "Sometimes it doesn't work right," he'd say. Sounded plausible. But a blade razor with the addition of shaving cream, now that spelled success. Each stroke of the razor along a creamy slathered face displayed indisputable evidence of its having been there by tell-tale paths of exposed skin. No more missed patches of facial hair. It seemed that a manually-propelled razor coupled with shaving cream was our answer.

On the other hand, there loomed an even more problematical aspect of razor usage. May I remind you once again that Jared's mental capacity does not match up to his chronological age. Ordinarily, when a razor is put in the hand of your average young teenage male for the first time, it's like a badge of courage. That razor symbolizes an honorary rite of passage. With razor in hand, he feels manly and proud, as did Jared. But said average teenager usually possesses an innate inclination to preserve life and limb. Putting a razor in the hand of a teen with a mental disability, however, is like giving a meat cleaver to a six year old and telling him to "have at it!" My conscience nagged me to boost up our health insurance coverage.

Thoughts of the challenge – boy versus blade – gave me a nervous rash and additional facial wrinkles. Jared's safety was paramount. There had to be a solution. Thank heavens there is such a thing as motherly instinct. What a wonderful thing! It gives us moms a built in psychological emergency kit that helps us instantly protect our children from harm. That instinct kicked in with a possible solution to the lethally sharp razor dilemma... I would shave him myself.

Okay – that thought lasted about two seconds. Deep respect for his self-esteem trumped the *safe* remedy. He would feel as if I were taking away his personal right to manliness, let alone the embarrassment of having his mommy wielding the blade. He deserved to feel as manly as every other manly guy. So, being a woman of the twentieth century, with experience, wisdom, and geared with a fair amount of feminine resourcefulness, I came up with a perfect plan – turn the job over to my husband. Once again, I am a genius.

Much to my relief, Lee became Jared's mentor of the blade. He did an admirable job, too. He went over the procedure several times (for repetition is key to Jared's ability to learn.) All the safety issues were addressed, all the important details were explained, and even a few of Lee's own specialized techniques were divulged. Jared was now officially one of the manly of the manly.

As time went by, Jared became quite proficient in the art of facial hair removal. The sideburns gave him a bit of a challenge, though. Lopsidedness occurred on occasion, but for the most part, he was very competent in the world of attaining manliness.

Ah, but there is always a fly in the ointment of routine things. In Jared's mind, there was some other hair on his face that probably would be fun to get rid of, too. We clueless parents hadn't thought of that scenario, and I was not prepared for the outcome.

At this point, I need to interject a reminder of what we, as the parents of Jared, had strived to accomplish in his upbringing. He happened to be an unbelievably fantastic human being in our eyes. And since we fully agreed with Coco Chanel, that "Adornment is never anything but a reflection of the self," we knew the importance of maintaining the appearance of a clean, well dressed, well groomed and well behaved young man who happened to have a mental handicap. Joe Q. Public's attitude and resultant acceptance toward said young man would depend upon those crucial elements, in our opinion.

It took effort, but we were determined to persevere to those ends. So when Jared sauntered downstairs to show me his "new look," I was not mentally prepared for the sight that would fill my visual screen.

I happen to be in the middle of my early morning workout routine in front of the TV sweating along with my mentor and physical idol, Jane Fonda. I seemed to be straining much more than she always seemed to be as she flaunted her polished and perfect physique on screen.

At the moment, I couldn't help but wonder why, after so many years of religiously performing this morning ritual, I was still a lot shorter, still not as flexible, and still quite a bit "fluffier" than perfect Miss Jane. While in deep philosophical contemplation over this incongruous phenomenon, a freshly showered-and-shaved Jared plopped down on the floor in front of me, a big pleased-with-himself smile gracing his newly renovated face.

As I struggled through the final few counts of the seemingly never ending leg lifts, I glanced at Jared. That was the onset of my coronary infarction. I honestly could feel my heart stop (and it was *not* a result of exercise). The person in front of me was a dead ringer for Freddy Krueger! Seriously! I am not trying to be over dramatic here. The actual visage of the grossly disfigured Freddie from Elm Street entered my head. (Come to think of it, I'm guessing Freddy's horrific facial deformity could very well have been a result of trying to rid himself of facial hair using those fingernails of his.) My sweet, handsome son with his full head of dark hair and his wonderfully dark eyebrows was now minus the eyebrows.

Have you ever seen a dark haired person minus the eyebrows? There is a reason for those things on one's face. They are not just there to protect the eyes from dust, dirt and sun. Nope. They are there to make one look human! Without them, I swear that Jared looked like one of Mr. Krueger's offspring.

At that moment, his innocent, pleased-with-himself smile didn't register in my head. I succumbed to a knee-jerk reaction; I screamed. It must have been a direct result of a subconscious angst about what others would think of my now weird-looking son. What started off as a pleased-with-himself smile turned into a look of confusion, then utter fear; the kind of fear that pre-empts tears. I think I fainted. I'm not sure. It's still a blur.

Even though eyebrows play a crucial role in protecting the eyes, there's an even more significant role that they play; they communicate expression – anger, surprise, joy, confusion, and so on. At the moment, my son looked like a blank sheet! What in the world was I going to do to make him look normal again!

Sadly, my initial reaction didn't take into consideration *his* initial reaction. Good-intentioned Mom was so worried over the radical change in his appearance that his feelings (evidenced by the transition from his pleased-with-himself expression to the look of shock and fear) didn't compute. We parents can be episodically dense. We can get so caught up in appropriateness and appearances that we forget what is really important – a child's feelings. Big lesson for me here. Knee jerk reactions show lack of control. They are reckless, not only damaging self-esteem, but damaging a lot of other things as well. Okay – lesson learned! I would never again fall prey to an unintentionally thoughtless reaction.

I apologized and hugged him. He forgave me for my initial

response, and we ultimately made it through that browless period, but not without effort. Every morning, like clockwork, I would artistically sketch faux eyebrows on Jared's face. And every day after school he would return home with brownish black smudges in the eyebrow vicinity.

Something surprising hit me. He never seemed concerned or affected in any way by that end-of-the-day strange, smudgy look. All right then – I decided I wouldn't be either. I *am* learning!

Side note: later on, well after his shaving training, Jared said something to his then eighty-nine year-old grandpa that I will never forget. We were eating dinner at a restaurant when I noticed Jared intently staring at Grandpa. He seemed to be studying his face. After a few minutes he said, "Grandpa, can I ask you a question?

"Sure thing, Jared. Shoot."

"So... how do you shave inside all those cracks?"

> *"...know thou, my son, that all these things shall give thee experience, which shall be for thy good." DC 122:7*

While home alone, Jared left this note on the door.

If anyone know's us
Or Jared - Come in,
If not Then leave now!
And specally
NO solicitators!

11

Christmas Unplugged

"To understand the heart and mind of a person, look not at what he has already achieved, but at what he aspires to do."
~ *Kahlil Gibran*

It was mid-afternoon and snowing outside. I was so content just relaxing in my comfy chair, looking out the window at the scraggly barren trees fighting to resist the white stuff. Eventually, they surrendered, transforming from stark nakedness into accepting a soft, stunning mantle of ethereal white. How remarkably exquisite! Nothing can compare with the magnificence and serene splendor of new fallen snow.

As I continued to savor the beauty of my surroundings, I noticed that the regal Utah pines seemed to actually welcome the delicate flakes. Those pine trees brought back a memory of a ten year-old Jared lumbering into the house with an armload of pinecones. "Mom! Let's go roast 'em!" I remembered being a bit confused and replied that I didn't know pinecones could be roasted. "Yeah, they can!" he said. "Like the song says, 'Pinecones roasting on an open fire.'" I chuckled to myself at the memory, and nestled deeper into my chair with my mug of steaming hot chocolate cradled in grateful fingers – and I reveled in the solace of the moment... *dolce fare niente.*

Pow! The door flew open, my reverie interrupted by a fifteen year-old Jared rushing into the room. His eyes glowed with uncontained excitement as he shared the news of his unusual school day. As he continued to churn out information, alarm and anxiety made an uneasy marriage in the pit of my stomach. Because I am the mother of Jared, it is a feeling not foreign to me.

ɢ৵

Back to the beginning of the day...

Jared was scheduled to take a field trip to the mall with his high school special education class. Since it was the Christmas season, the teacher must have felt it would be a prime opportunity to mix the Christmas spirit with a learning experience in math (specifically, checkbook maintenance). I was not aware of this field trip for some odd reason. And since I did not know about it, I was also not privy to the checkbook that must accompany said field trip. Had I been aware, I would have added a few more dollars to Jared's checking account. As it stood, he had a grand total of $2.50. You can't even buy good popcorn for $2.50! Keep in mind that back then, automatic overdraft protection had not been invented. If he wrote a check for more than $2.50, it meant he would be a big red overdrawn in his brand-spanking-new checking account. The ugly result: a bounced check for a first-time checkbook user. (Huge lesson here: at times, life gifts us with lemons.)

Just a few weeks earlier I had opened the checking account for Jared. I figured that sooner or later we would teach him how to use it. At this point in time, however, Jared was a novice in checking account savoir-faire. He wasn't even sure what a checking account was. Accordingly, he had not a clue what the terms *balance* or *deposit* meant. (It could be that he inherited that from me.)

The other side of checking account expertise involved the check-writing skill. Now that was a horse of a different color! Jared knew about check-writing. After all, hadn't he seen me write a gazillion checks over the years? But to Jared, writing a check and having money in the bank had no correlation. Evidently, in Jared's head, one only need write a check and voilà, the magical money fairy took care of it.

What Jared did know, however, was that he was the proud

owner of a nifty checkbook. And not only did he own one, he had lots and lots of checks in it. He felt fully prepared for this day's adventure. He also knew one more relatively important thing: he was never supposed to touch said checkbook without permission. But it didn't take a rocket scientist to figure out Jared's reasoning for taking it anyway, "My teacher *told* me to." (Like I said, lemons.)

At this point, a little background might be helpful. Even though Jared has Down syndrome, he functions remarkably well socially. Sociality seems to be his forte. (This, we feel, was inherited from his grandparents. Thank goodness for genes!) But just as we are all quite diverse in our various talents and abilities, Jared is also diverse. Socially he is gifted. Math and logic, there's the rub.

My own downfall is technology, specifically anything with an electrical cord coming out of it. But the Internet, I get. Using that mode I found several creative web sites to help Jared work on his math skills. I am happy to report that he is doing much better in that area. Unfortunately, there are no logic drills that supplement computer beginner math exercises. And unless one knows Jared really, really well, the lack-of-logic thing slips through the cracks. Running true to form, no one on the Christmas field trip team realized Jared's lack of logic or knowledge regarding checkbook savvy.

To further frustrate the possibility of a field trip without incident, that particular day a substitute teacher was at the helm. *A sub on a field trip!* (Lemons)

The field trip was underway. Once at the mall, the sub partnered the students up with their peer tutor buddies before turning everyone loose. Jared, however, ended up odd man out, so the sub allowed him to "go it alone" – after all, he seemed *so capable.* (Lemons, lemons, lemons!)

The first store he ventured into led him straight to a jewelry department. A lovely pearl necklace caught his eye. His benevolent sweet spirit took over (in addition to his checkbook screaming to be used.) What a way cool present for his Aunt Mike for Christmas. The $59.95 price tag didn't mean squat. After all, he had *his checkbook.* The check was written, the pearl necklace bought, and a thrilled Jared strode out of the store.

The next establishment he came to was a menswear store. Wasn't his older cousin, Trent, getting ready to go on an LDS mission? Didn't he need a suit? After Jared waved down a salesman and showed him the handsome suit he wanted to purchase for his cousin, said salesman (bless his wise heart) suggested that Jared bring Trent in for a fitting before buying the suit. That wonderful astute man saved us much financial grief. The necklace, however, was still on the books.

We now pick up the story – me in my comfy chair holding my mug of hot chocolate listening to Jared finish off the details of his field trip. He beamed as he showed me the purchase he had made with his handy dandy, now overdrawn, checkbook: an elegant, and according to his checking account, very lethal necklace. He finished his chronicle by telling me he had picked out a really cool suit for Trent. Because I was in extreme shock, I misconstrued his report and thought he had already bought the suit. (Lemons, shemmons! We're talking grapefruits here!)

This is where being a parent gets tricky. In that instant of off-the-charts flabbergastation, it is a given rule that parents go bonkers. Kids wait for it. They expect it. My initial gut response was to let my eyes bug out, my jaw drop, then rub my genie bottle to wish for instant funds to magically appear in the account that would cover the cost of the necklace and suit. But with sixteen years of parenting under my belt (and learning from the experience of my reaction to his shaving-his-eyebrows-off event) I'd like to think that I have gained a little ground in self control.

Early on, I'd always thought that in this world there were very good reasons for going momentarily insane. However, during these later years, I've learned that it solves nothing – except adding plaque to my arteries. I only hesitated a few seconds (enough time to breathe), then I threw my arms around my hugely enthusiastic son and told him what an angel he was for selecting such wonderful and thoughtful gifts for his aunt and cousin.

He straightened me out on the suit purchase (there is a God

in heaven!) but there was still a proverbial fly in the ointment: the expensive necklace must be returned. Jared ended up picking out a more appropriately priced gift *after* a trip to the bank and a short lesson on economics. He even got to write a check for it.

I'm happy to report that things turned out well. Aunt Mike was thrilled with Jared's gift of a beautiful stone soap dish that she has on display in her bathroom still today. And we were able to educate Jared about checking accounts and checkbooks. (Just to be on the safe side, however, the vote was to bury the checkbook for a few years.)

"Reproving betimes [before it is too late] *with sharpness* [clarity], *when moved upon by the Holy Ghost; and then showing forth afterwards an increase of love toward him whom thou hast reproved, lest he esteem thee to be his enemy;" D&C 121:43*

I was sitting in the car, impatiently waiting for Jared,
becoming more annoyed by the second and thumb-tapping
the steering wheel when he finally got in the car.

"Oh, sorry Mom. I'm really trying not to wobble. (dawdle)
It's just that I feel a little largistic today." (lethargic)

12

I'm Okay, You're Okay

"I testify that as we mature spiritually under the guidance of the Holy Ghost, our sense of personal worth, of belonging, and of identity increases." ~ James E. Faust

Some of my most profound lessons have come from Jared's reaction to everyday things. One of the most valued lessons came from a driveway basketball game (DWB) he happened to be playing with a neighbor boy, whom I will call Dufus.

Our driveway was no stranger to the hours and hours of athletic shoe pounding it took from Jared, John, their dad, and various neighborhood all-star wannabes as they honed their dribbling, shooting, and chasing-the-runaway-ball-down-the-street skills. They loved DWB (except the chasing-the-ball part.) They probably would have preferred a nice wooden floor court over our concrete driveway, but our driveway was available 24/7, and it was free. No brainer.

When you picture a home style basketball hoop, you usually picture a hoop attached to a portable standard located somewhere on the driveway. Ours wasn't. We had to be resourceful. Our driveway was scrunched for space. So my inventive husband and his clever brother, Bill, ingeniously mounted our hoop on our balcony railing directly over the center of the driveway. It turned out to be a great location ...except for one slight drawback: anytime the ball hit the hoop or even the backboard (which, I understand, is the object of trying to make baskets), it twanged the railing which in turn vibrated the entire balcony which happened to be attached to our master bedroom. Hence, my cherished naps always had to take a backseat to DWB. I tried taking a nap once during a hot DWB game, and it nearly rattled my brain right out of my skull.

Jared was about fourteen, though mentally younger, and Dufus was the same age as our younger son, John – about twelve, and at least a head taller than Jared. Dufus didn't happen to be my favorite in terms of neighborhood kids. You might be familiar with the type: *occasionally* truthful, *occasionally* civil, *occasionally* combed his hair, and *always* had a sort of shifty look. John was absent for that day's DWB game for some reason – probably out somewhere working on a merit badge. It was just Dufus and Jared, one-on-one.

I happened to be in the master bedroom changing the sheets on our bed, vibrating with each successful shot. The large sliding glass door was open, both to let in the fresh spring air and keep me within earshot of my son and our dubious neighborhood ne'er-do-well. Jared and Dufus were having a good old time – a perfect day for DWB. I could hear bits and pieces of their basketball banter and things actually seemed to be on the up and up. But then Dufus, living up to his reputation, had to screw things up. He said something that made my blood boil. Loudly and clearly he blurted out, "You're dumb, aren't you?"

I'm sure you've heard how a mother bear will, without reservation, savagely kill to protect her cub. Momma bear had nothing on me. I was ready to slide open that screen door, leap over the balcony to the driveway below, box Dufus' ears, and maybe send him to another planet. The word *angry* didn't cover it. I had never experienced such a consuming type of mad.

The only thing that saved Dufus from being jammed through our basketball hoop was a momentary 'what if' thought. *What if* something like this is said to Jared and I'm not around. What then? There would not always be a knight in shining armor to come to his rescue when unkind words are said or unkind things are done. I knew I needed to let my son handle the situation.

While raising him, we had given him some tools to deal with circumstances exactly like this. But would he remember? Would he be hurt? Would he be angry? I was eager beyond words to hear his response. (This is one of those moments when the few gray hairs already on one's head multiply like rabbits on fertility drugs.) I hated not being able to step in and "fix this." I could hardly breathe. I just stood out of sight, fists clenched, anxiously waiting for Jared to speak. (*Parental torture* – I think it is called.)

I kept waiting …and waiting. The ball kept bouncing. It kept hitting the backboard. Jared didn't say anything. Not a word. Dufus didn't say anything either. The ball kept bouncing. Then the banter began again as if that terrible phrase had never been uttered. Everything was back to normal. I was stunned. Jared had let that remark roll off him like water off a duck's back. We had taught him early on the "sticks and stones" thing, but to actually witness the use of it at that key moment was awesome. How many times had I not followed my own advice? How many times had *I* bit back when someone nipped at me? Here was my sweet son, teaching me, showing me, the best way to handle a Dufus. Water off a duck's back. I was awestruck. I was humbled.

Maybe he was able to handle the situation so well because he was so self-confident. I'd like to think that being kindhearted and forgiving played a part. But I really believe that he just honestly feels good about himself. He likes himself. He figures everyone else must like him, too. After all, God loves him just as he is, doesn't He? Then why even let cruel or thoughtless remarks in?

That type of self-esteem kept cropping up throughout his life. Like when he had his doctor appointment for the scout camp physical. He was in his twenties at the time. When his name was called in the waiting room, we dutifully followed Nurse Efficient's lead toward the exam room. Nurse Efficient stood aside as she opened the exam room door. Gentleman that he is, Jared allowed me to enter first.

Nurse Efficient immediately noticed from Jared's chart that it had been quite a while since he had had a complete physical examination and that the doctor would need a urine sample for this occasion. Before he could step foot in the exam room she spun him around and guided him down the hall to the restroom. I settled myself in a rather comfy exam room chair, and waited.

Since Nurse Efficient was, well ….efficient, *obviously* she would be able to see that Jared had Down syndrome, so *obviously* she would take care of my son and instruct him on the procedure of producing a urine sample – *obviously*. Besides, I was in the mode of backing off the "mommy" role, and stoically trying to let my grown-up son handle more grown-up things solo. Most of the time, if he didn't understand something, he would usually ask for help. It didn't really matter, though, because I figured Nurse Efficient would do right by him. I figured wrong.

It didn't take long before the exam room door opened. In scurried Jared who plopped down on the examination table. Nurse Efficient closed the door. Though I'm somewhat backing off the "mommy" thing, I'm still responsible for a certain amount of follow-up, so I said, "It's been a while since you've had to do that urine sample thing, huh?"

"Yeah."

"Did the nurse help you remember what to do?"

"No."

(Oh boy)

"Were you able to figure it out yourself?"

"Yeah,"

(Whew)

"…but it was a little hard."

The phrase *"a little hard"* concerned me. What would be *"hard"* about producing a urine sample? Over the years, through a myriad of those experiences, I have had the opportunity to sharpen my skills of not overreacting. I am very proud of my non-overreacting competence. So with my best nonchalant demeanor, I casually asked, "Just what do you mean by *hard,* sweetie?"

"Well," he said, "I had to go really bad, so it was really hard."

Though my angst was mounting, as I said before, I am a master at duplicity. I should win some type of an award for demonstrating my faux nonchalance. Thus, in full-casual mode, I asked, "What do you think was so hard about it, honey?"

He said, "Well, I had to go really, really bad. So I filled up six of those little cups."

Holding my breath ….holding ….holding …trying to stay in complete control. May I humbly state that I have not only polished my skills of hiding concern and worry, but of suppressing out and out guffaws at inappropriate times. If I were to let laughter loose at this moment, Jared's self-esteem might take a hit. Biting the inside of my cheek helps a lot. With a totally straight face I said, "You know, honey, from past experience, I think you only need to fill one of those little cups — the rest you can just deposit directly in the toilet."

At this point, most of us might feel mortified, or at the very least, a little embarrassed for having filled six cups when only one was needed. But here is where Jared rises to the top of the self-esteem scale. Feeling totally comfortable and pleased with his performance, his comment was, "Then they're *really* going to happy with what *I* left them!"

That was too great! How I wish I had that iron-clad self-assurance! It's something I intend to work on.

Afterword, I couldn't help but chuckle inside, though, as I pictured the lab technician's face when she opened that little lab door in the wall to find six full specimen cups sitting on the sill from just one person.

There might be times, however, that you could interpret Jared as being a little *too* confident. For most folks that would be synonymous with arrogance or conceit, but Jared is the exception to that rule. Jared is anything but arrogant, and certainly not conceited. It's just that he has such an absolutely solid sense of self-worth. He feels so comfortable with who he is.

Do not confuse self-importance with self-worth. There is a world of difference. And what's more, I sincerely believe that the unintentional humor (that seems to be his verdant companion) is a result of the fact that he does have such a strong sense of self-worth. The inadvertent humor just happens to be a wonderfully endearing byproduct.

I'll admit there was a time I worried he might be headed in the vanity direction. It sort of snuck up on both of us. It happened during the time that Jared performed with a group called PALS (Performing Artists Lengthening Strides). The director of that group was a wonderful man (a retired actor/singer) who, because of his genuine benevolence, organized this group of all special needs kids after he retired from Hollywood and moved to Utah. (Smart man) His experience and expertise afforded him the ability to convert songs and dance routines from musicals to fit the kids' ability levels. He was a master at it – and he loved it. The group performed all over the state, and then some. It was an outstanding experience for the kids; it built self-esteem, self-confidence, self-discipline, poise, and talent. It also touched the hearts of the audiences who responded with tears of joy, admiration, and standing ovations. It was a win-win situation.

As time rolled on the kids got better and better, practice times increased, and so did the performance dates. The effort we spent on PALS began to consume massive amounts of time and that green stuff. It was when it started to wear on me that I began to regain my objectivity. Red flags were waving everywhere in my head. I was able to finally see the effect it was having on Jared, and I didn't like it.

During those performances Jared was not only getting applause, he was getting huge amounts of attention, praise, and notoriety. For him, it was heaven. He loved it! But I don't think any parent alive wants their kid to become bigheaded or full of himself. He wasn't egotistical or self-absorbed *yet*, but I could see it coming. We had a serious sit-down talk about it. To my surprise, he understood the point I was trying to make. He, too, was able to see the danger zones. At first, I think he was actually more concerned that I was concerned. (I am so grateful that he respects my judgment.) He made the decision to quit PALS and focus on things that would not only help himself, but help others as well; scouting, volunteer work, church activities, serving elderly neighbors, etc.

Focusing on these things gave Jared enormous pleasure. His focus turned away from himself to include those around him. It not only fostered a love and respect for others, it even increased his feeling of self-worth. There were times, however, that he was still able to be in the performance spotlight, but it wasn't with PALs. He allowed Cooper (our furry family member) and me to tag along to nursing homes and care centers where we entertained the sweet folks there. (He didn't even mind that Cooper got most of the applause.)

Throughout Jared's life, Lee and I weren't the only ones intent on building his self-esteem. Our entire extended family rallied to support Jared from the day he was born. For example: about a month or so after Jared entered our lives on August 24, 1977, I was scheduled to return to teaching and coaching at the university in October. Just the thought of leaving my darling new baby in order to go back to work made me an emotional wreck, especially since he was my first child. And as a first-time mother, I was already one huge wobbly ball of emotions, nerves, and cluelessness. I felt I needed every available minute to get to know my son, to help him in every way possible, and to figure out this motherhood gig.

There were also other issues involved that made it hard to tear myself away from my sweet new son. Jared had daily exercises he had to do. No, this was not because I was an overzealous PE teacher making my infant son do push-ups and squat-thrusts. Due to his handicap, he was visited weekly by an early intervention nurse from the state. During every visit she would assess his needs then assign daily exercises for him that were to be done several times a day to stimulate him mentally and to help strengthen his flaccid muscle tone (which is common in children with Down syndrome).

My emotions would have been off the charts if I would have had to leave my special needs infant son in the hands of a complete stranger or a daycare worker with all the extra care and attention he required. But I had an earthly angel: my mother. She not only volunteered to take on the responsibility, but was thrilled about it.

Bless her!

The time was nearing for me to return to work and Mom could hardly wait to get started with "Little Pants" (as she called him). Her eagerness made me love her even more. Life, however, throws us curves when we least expect it, does it not? That curve came in the form of a wrenched back. Mom was laid up! The doc told her she shouldn't lift anything heavier than a paper clip for several months. Jared weighed more than a paper clip. But Mom never flinched. She already had a solution up her sleeve. She hired a woman to do the lifting and carrying for her until her back healed. What a woman! Like I said, earthly angel.

It was that type of total support we experienced all through Jared's life, like my dad's relationship with Jared. They were best buddies. They became even closer after my mother passed away. Jared was twenty-five at the time. Those two spent a lot of time together – and still do. They're perfect for each other: Jared offers muscle to help with heavy-lifting type favors, and offers devoted companionship to a ninety-plus Grandpa; Grandpa brings his wisdom, knowledge, special stories, and a listening ear to the table for Jared. It's a beautiful match.

On one occasion my dad tried to tutor Jared a little while they were cruising in Grandpa's substantially large, cranberry red, seats of soft kid-skin leather, very roomy, 1997 Lincoln Town Car that rides like a cabin cruiser on a smooth sea. It's a beauty. Jared thoroughly enjoys his outings with Grandpa in his grand car.

That day they were taking a trip out to my sister's place about 30 miles south. Grandpa figured he'd test Jared to see if he remembered the way to his Aunt Mike's, and to see if he could describe the route. On the highway a couple of miles from her street, Grandpa asked Jared to give him directions to Mike's house from that point. Jared thought about it for a minute, and said, "Go straight for a while and then turn _left_ at the big yellow house on the corner."

This was not correct. The correct route would be to go straight for a while and then turn _right_ at the big yellow house on the corner.

Grandpa said, "Are you *sure we* should turn *left*?"

Jared replied confidently, "I am *sure* that we should turn *left* at the big yellow house on the corner, Grandpa."

Grandpa asked again, "Are you absolutely positively certain?" (Which is his way of saying you are wrong, so change your story.) But Jared was sticking to his guns and wouldn't budge with the left turn deal. Then Grandpa figured he'd better ask another question, "Jared, do you know which is your right side and which is your left side?"

Jared nodded enthusiastically, though his reasoning turned out to be somewhat skiwampus. Jared gave a demonstration to prove his point; he lifted his right arm high in that big roomy car and said, "This is my right side." Then he lifted his left arm and stated, "This is my left side." So far he was right on the money, but he wasn't finished. He continued by making a pointy finger with his raised *left* hand, crossing it over in front of himself, pointing to the *right* side with said left hand and asserted, "...see, you turn *left*." Grandpa chose not to argue with this logic.

That was just one out of many humorous-type Jared events.

This leads me to tell you that I am very grateful for two things: I acknowledged my memory impediment years ago, so I always took notes on all those humorous Jared events immediately after they happened on whatever was handy; pieces of scrap paper, napkins, the back of business cards or receipts, the car registration, the palm of my hand, etc. I have a file full of an assortment of weird paper-type stuff with Jared gems written on them. Whenever I needed a good laugh, I'd always go to my files and pull out a few and read them.

And the second thing I have learned from them all is that Jared's inadvertent humor is the best shock absorber this life has to offer. He has brought more humor and laughter into my life than I would have ever thought possible. And besides, he always laughs at my jokes. What more could a mother want?

"The worth of souls is great in the sight of God." DC 18:10

Back in high school, Jared was asked by his teacher what he wanted to do after graduation.
Thinking about this for only a few seconds, he confidently declared,

"I want to shovel manure at Ron's Barber Shop."

Point of clarification:
Jared's longtime barber, Ron, happened to own several horses as well as a very large barn next to his barber shop that housed said horses.
(The irony should not be missed.)

13

The Miracle

"The ultimate measure of a man is not where he stands in moments of comfort and convenience, but where he stands at times of challenge and controversy." ~ *Dr. Martin Luther King*

There are times when certain things we experience in this life impact our psyche so substantially that they change us forever. There are things we know, and then there are things we believe. In harmony with that assertion, there are times when an experience overwhelmingly and emphatically confirms a belief we've always had. For me, this experience brought with it physical proof of something I believed early on; children, especially those with disabilities, have a strong and very special connection to God.

The experience of which I speak began in Jared's early years. He had more than his share of regular childhood illnesses, and of longer duration with each. This was no surprise. It is typical of children with Downs. From all the literature I had read, kids with Downs are predisposed to immunodeficiency. Evidently, their "Killer T cells" aren't up to par, which simply put means their immune systems tend to be slackers. But the most devastating and rather unusual medical challenge Jared faced showed up at age four.

When Jared turned four years old, we noticed that he started having difficulty walking. He was showing signs that something in his leg was hurting. We took him to his regular GP who referred us to an orthopedic surgeon. After x-rays were taken, they confirmed the specialist's initial diagnosis: Legg Perthes disease. This time Down syndrome had nothing to do with this strange new condition, it just complicated things.

We had never heard of this disease. The doctor explained that the femoral head (the ball of the upper leg bone) was dying. Whoa. Something dying in one of Jared's bones sounded bad! (I could feel a whole new set of pesky grey hairs gaining new territory.) He went on to reassure us that it wasn't life-threatening or incurable, but would take *several years* to heal. (*Several years*?) He explained that it was crucial that the femoral head not experience any trauma or jarring during the healing process. In other words, we were warned not to let Jared run, skip, hop or jump. (*For several years? Was he kidding?*) Tell that to a four year old boy! How in the world were we supposed to keep an active little boy from running, hopping and jumping? The only positive in that disturbing news was the *skipping* part. Jared did not know how to skip. That's a pretty lame positive. Just thinking about what was in store made my head throb.

The next couple of years were frustrating for Jared and exasperating for Lee and me. We were like vigilant mother hens on steady guard duty trying to watch Jared's every move so that he wouldn't do anything that might injure the fragile, soft bone tissue. We petitioned the neighbors, extended family members, Jared's teachers, and even our little three year-old John to join our Mother Hen Squad. In Jared's eyes, we were all sort of the bad guys, stopping him from doing the things he loved most. He didn't hate us for it, but he certainly wasn't happy. In fact, he was more than a little miffed. (More grey hairs)

Two years after the initial diagnosis, the condition of the femoral head had deteriorated. This was the scenario we had been dreading – the onset of a leg brace. By design, it would keep the now mushy tip of the femoral head in a "safe" position within the hip socket. The brace would be strapped to his rather short, typically Downs legs. Yes, *legs* – as in both!

When the doc first mentioned "brace," what initially came to mind was absolutely nothing like the actual contraption. It turned out to be a grotesque apparatus from Hades that would make Jared's life as a typically active young boy impossible to experience. It restricted every type of normal body movement. He hated it. I hated it. We all hated it. Unfortunately, it was absolutely necessary.

For those of you who know ballet, the position Jared had to endure with his brace on was like being stuck in a wide second plié – for those of you who are not ballet buffs, it was a stance which closely resembled that of riding a very short, extremely obese horse, only without the horse.

The brace was made of stainless steel with a thick two inch wide heavy leather waistband. Two metal posts extended from the waistband down each leg and attached to even wider leather straps just above the knee to hold it in place. The kicker was the post in the middle. It connected to both leg posts on the thigh straps keeping his legs wide apart. The only way he could walk was to perform an exaggerated waddle back and forth; first leaning way over to one side on one leg, swing the other leg a little forward, and then leaning way over to the other side to transfer his weight to the other leg, and so on, to progress forward. He actually looked a little scary coming directly at you if you didn't know the whole story. His walk resembled the way I played "scary monster" with our dog.

As I've mention before, we always did our best to make sure Jared always looked nice, neat, and pinchably cute. But now, with this ugly leg brace thingamajig, he looked strange, even a little menacing; not what we had in mind for setting the stage for a fresh and bright physical exterior.

If the appearance of the brace wasn't bad enough, it came with a suspiciously weird noise; it made a squeaky click-clacking noise when he walked (or, I should say, hobbled). We tried a liberal dose of WD-40. It didn't work. He sounded like a loud squeaky version of Tin Man in the Wizard of Oz.

My heart seemed to be stuck in my throat through most of the three years he had to wear it. And the restrictions it presented were tough to handle; he couldn't go down a slippery slide, ride a tricycle, swing in a swing, or even play in a sand pile because the sand would accumulate under the straps. He couldn't bounce a ball, hit a ball, or kick a ball. He had difficulty just standing up, sitting down, or walking. I was left with a lump in my throat watching him trying to make it up the school bus steps every weekday morning.

There was an additional crummy drawback to the brace; it was the staring and odd looks from strangers. After Jared was born, we had learned how to deal with the staring in a positive way. Now, with this strange looking gizmo, coupled with an already noticeable condition, we could see this as a potential self-esteem breaker for Jared. We decided the best course of action was to let Jared, himself, handle the situation. We told him that if he ever felt uncomfortable when someone began staring at him in his brace, we instructed *him* to tell them that the brace was to help his leg get better. It worked. We are geniuses.

As a matter of fact, it turned into a very positive tool. I got such a kick out of watching the expression on the faces of those who got caught staring. As a rule, they usually had not been aware they had been staring. But when Jared spoke up to explain, "This is my brace that helps my leg heal," they first would be mortified, and turn bright red for having been caught. But then they always responded kindly and with interest. That tool was win-win: he felt better for having explained his weird appearance, and they would be more mindful of not staring in the future.

But through the difficulty, the restrictions, and the pain; through the 30-plus x-rays, and through all the discomfort and misery of wearing that ghastly brace, he remained even tempered, positive, and uncomplaining. If I had been in his position, I would've been major ticked-off. I would have been ranting, venting to friends and neighbors, writing to complain to my congressman and the president – but not Jared. That is, not until *D-day*.

Jared's D-day was the day that his last-straw hit the bale; the day he finally gave in and just couldn't take it anymore. It happened on an overcast April afternoon in 1985. For the months and months he had to wear that thing he had been such a trooper, until that day.

Every month or two, like clockwork, we would visit the doc

to have x-rays taken. The doc would bring the x-rays into the exam room, pop them up in front of the display light, point to the unchanged appearance of the femur head, and then tell Jared that he was sorry, but his bone was still "mushy." The brace would have to be worn a while longer. Jared was a little disappointed each time, but he snapped right out of it – but not on D-day.

D-day came as a result of his February doctor visit where the doc happened to mention, offhandedly, that he sure hoped the bone would heal before our next x-ray visit to him so that when summer arrived, a now seven year-old Jared might be able to get rid of the brace. I don't know why the doctor said that, because I could see absolutely no change whatsoever in the current x-rays. If the truth were known, neither could he. I really believe that he just wanted to deliver some type of positive news for a sad little Jared. Big mistake on his part.

So two months later, on an April day, this *D-day* visit, Jared had been thinking about what the doc had said at the end of the last February visit – the part where he *hoped* Jared's bone would heal for summer. Jared's hopes were now way, way up. Exorbitantly up. He was positive the doc would finally give him permission to take the brace off in time for summer. At long last he would be able to have a decent, fun summer without that hot, cumbersome, ugly old brace restricting him from all the fun activities that he loved.

The doc performed the same routine ritual of whisking into the exam room and popping the x-rays into the clips to hold them in front of the display light. My heart sank. I could see that there was absolutely no change. The doctor had no idea that Jared's hopes were so high on this particular visit. So he, once again, informed Jared in a grim voice that the brace would have to remain in place. He said he was sure sorry the x-rays didn't look better, and then he scurried out of the room.

The room fell silent. Jared's face was pale. He looked lost and confused. He had been so sure that the news was going to be good this time. It was anything but.

Seeing him this way was almost unbearable. Up to this time

he had been such a good little sport about the whole rotten deal. There was nothing left for me to say. I had said it all during prior visits to boost his morale. Now, I could think of nothing that would lessen his disillusionment. We quietly strapped on the brace and left the office.

On the way home I kept trying to get him focused on something else. I needed to try to lift his spirits, if only a little. It wasn't working. He didn't even want to get an ice cream cone, get pizza, or go to a movie. There was just nothing I could do or say that made any difference. To be truthful, I felt just as crummy as he did. I almost hated that doctor for not having some good news for us.

We got home, went inside the house, and resumed our usual activities for the remainder of the day. I headed for the kitchen to start dinner, and Jared hobbled toward the recreation room to watch TV with our now six year-old John.

After a while, I thought I'd better go check on him. He wasn't in the rec room. I asked John where Jared was, but he didn't know. I called throughout the house. No answer. I checked the bathrooms – no luck. The playroom was empty. I was growing more concerned by the minute due to the bad news he had to digest that afternoon. He was nowhere in the house.

I went outside and started calling his name. Again, no answer. This wasn't like Jared. I became frantic. I started racing around the outside of the house looking for any trace of him. Just as I was about ready to lose my mind from worry, I finally spotted him. He was sitting on the grass at the corner of the house next to the fence. I ran over to him, ready to lash out and give him the dreaded pointy-finger lecture for not answering me, but felt constrained. I so wanted to throttle the little stinker for scaring the beejeebers out of me! But again, I felt compelled not to dive into a foray of frantic jabber. Instead, I quietly sat down next to him.

He was sitting there, pulling handfuls of grass out of the lawn. He just kept pulling and tossing, pulling and tossing. I put my arm around him, and after a few minutes, felt I could speak. I asked, "Want to tell me about it, sweetie?"

Though he appeared to be crestfallen, he also looked very, very angry. That, too, was uncharacteristic for Jared. He just kept pulling out the grass. Then, without looking up, he firmly and angrily announced, "I'm talking to Heavenly Father!"

I thought that was the perfect thing for him to be doing after such news. I had a pretty good idea what he might be saying, but I wanted to wait for Jared to talk it through. I sat quietly, waiting.

Finally he said, "I'm telling Him I want my brace off!"

We had taught Jared how to pray, so the "telling Him" part caught me a little off guard. One does not usually *tell* Heavenly Father to do anything. One *asks*. I'm picturing lightning bolts shooting down from above. But Heavenly Father knew Jared better than I did, and loved him just as much, probably more. He knew his heart. I knew He would grant Jared a little leeway concerning proper prayer etiquette. He, more than anyone, understood Jared's frame of mind. I hugged Jared, told him I loved him, and helped him back into the house.

A little over a month after the June D-day visit, Jared and I entered the doc's exam room once again. This time, the doc burst through the door, popped the x-rays in front of the display light, and pointed to the hip joint. He said, "Look at this. Just look at this! It's unbelievable! I've never seen anything like this before. The time frame from your last visit doesn't match what I'm seeing on the x-ray, but the x-ray shows that the femur head is almost totally healed."

I looked closely at the x-ray. I was stunned. The femur head was solid. It had only been a few weeks since we had seen the "mushy" one. I smiled. Jared literally cheered out loud.

The doctor told him to get rid of the brace and to have a fabulous summer. "Thanks" just doesn't cover it to a benevolent Father in Heaven who knew the heart and heard the prayer of a very sad, yet very courageous young boy. The miracle came "after much tribulation."

"And all things, whatsoever ye shall ask in prayer, believing, ye shall receive." *Matthew 21:22*

Jared's Crooked Cliché

"It just came to me, right out of the clean blue air."

(out of the clear blue sky)

14

IQ... SQ, PQ, AQ, ULQ...

"God did not people the earth with a vibrant orchestra of personalities only to value the piccolos of the world."
~ Joseph B. Wirthlin

What is it about IQ anyway? I'll just bet my last piece of cherry covered cheesecake that you probably felt the same way about it as I did growing up. It wasn't necessarily a measurement of intelligence. In reality, it was an evaluation tool. In school, the kids who had high IQs were admired, and not just by me – by almost everybody, including teachers. They were not only admired, they were revered. An instant respect materialized just being in their presence.

But let's be truthful – we kids with average IOs were just a little jealous of their gift of supersonic intelligence. While it was true that we robotically respected the high IQ kids, we average IQ kids felt just a little slighted. There always seemed to be ever ready praise for their flashy academic achievements. They were the ones who received all those impressive awards at yearend assemblies. (Though I shouldn't complain; I think I received an award for perfect attendance once.) Those brilliant kids were the teachers' pets, the ones the teachers called on most, the ones who got to write on the chalk board, the ones who got into universities scot free. I always felt that was a crummy deal. The cold hard fact was that absolutely no special training was required, no exemplary effort was needed on behalf of those folks with those sky-scraping IQs – it was automatic! It came with conception!

Everything in academia was a walk in the park for those smarty-pants kids. Dang their hides! For the rest of us average-type kids, we had to work our little tails off.

As I grew out of my teens, I let jealousy go and maintained a hefty respect for those super-stellar citizens. And when I was hired by the university, I was even more in awe of those who were my supremely intelligent colleagues – well, at least most of them. There were always those few who were a bit pompous, sometimes arrogant, and often times condescending. (For some reason, those traits seem to accompany a few brainy professors.) But the majority of high IQers were instantly and unquestionably respected by me. And then along came cute little Jared who threw my fundamental high IQ view into a tailspin.

After being around Jared the first few years of his life, I became aware of some rather unbelievable qualities that he possessed. As those qualities surfaced, I realized that my view of IQ all those years had been skewed. It occurred to me that a high IQ shouldn't qualify a person for automatic respect, instant admiration, or by golly, even likeableness! As a matter of fact, there were a few pretty smart people I knew who were very unlikeable. Though they were off-the-charts smart, they were low in other areas, like benevolence, common sense, humor, patience, understanding, or kindness. The more I was around Jared, the more I became aware of a whole new array of significant "quotient" categories that never get any credit. That, dear friends, is a travesty.

Let me share some other significant Qs with you. One of my good friends, Kathy, had an extremely high GQ – Guts Quotient. She had more backbone than a herculean rat in a pen of angry gorillas. For example, when she was in junior high, she took a school bus out for a joy ride. It wouldn't have gotten her into so much trouble if it hadn't had the entire pep club on board at the time. (Her CSQ – Common Sense Quotient – was a little on the low side.) But were it not for her exceptionally high GQ, she and I and another friend, Debbie, would still to this day be wandering around lost in a cave licking water off walls to stay alive.

Kathy's motto in life was, '*Where there is dicey adventure, there go I'.* Her entire life encompassed one adventure after another. Even when we got to college it hadn't diminished one single molecule.

One day between quarters, she called Deb and me to set up a spelunking escapade in an infamously cavernous cave in a nearby canyon. Even though we had slipped brand new batteries in our flashlights beforehand, they started to lose power halfway through our spelunking. We decided to turn back, but not in time.

We resorted to using just one flashlight at a time to conserve what collective battery life we had left, but one by one they bit the dust. After the weak beam from the last flashlight petered out we were trapped in a sea of darkness. The cave entrance was still at least a half mile away.

There we stood in total blackness. We couldn't even speak. We were terrified. The only sound was the echo of the incessant drip-drip-dripping of cave water all around us.

We were surrounded by the musty smell of the damp dirt floor, and periodically we felt the muffled whoosh of too-close-for-comfort bat wings. We shivered as the cave's chronic damp chill penetrated us to the bone. We were beyond petrified. Had I been prone to be a screamer, I would have screamed my lungs out.

But then there was Kathy with her off-the-charts GQ. She took over. When she told us that if we grabbed on to each other's shirttails, she would lead us out, we both thought she was out of her adventurous mind. However, the alternative was to sit on cold wet dirty rock, start sobbing, and eat dirt.

Deb and I gave in. We grabbed each other's shirttails and Kathy led the way; sometimes crawling on hands and knees, sometimes slithering, sometimes scooting on our backsides along angular floors, having no idea if we were close to one of the deep drop-offs or entering one of the many offshoots which would lead us even deeper into the cave's entrails instead of out. Because I am writing this book, you can guess the outcome. Thank heavens her

GQ had been far superior to ours. Bless her little GQ heart.

Then there is SQ – Social Quotient. Jared happens to have a very high SQ. Like those with high IQ, I believe he, too, came that way. It was probably inherited from my parents, since my dad is an extremely well-liked person. He is friendly to everyone and fairly gregarious, though not as gregarious as was my mother. Her affableness sometimes drove my dad a little nuts. Like the time they were eating in a restaurant and my mother noticed a couple sitting at another table, and said, "Hey, that couple over there looks really nice. Why don't we invite them to come over to our table?" Dad cringed. He didn't happen to be that affable.

There was one instance where she and Dad were at a party where a band was playing. At the end of the party in the wee hours of the morning she figured the guys in the band might be hungry, so she invited the entire band over to our house for scrambled eggs and bacon – her SQ was in the gargantuan range!

As I said, Jared has this uncanny knack of sociability. The wonderful byproduct of that is that he genuinely likes everyone, and he sincerely cares about everyone – a super high CQ – Care Quotient. Just like the time he and I took Grandpa out to dinner. After we finished eating, we walked out the front door of the restaurant and noticed we were minus Jared. (This is not uncommon. We find that Jared likes to stick around and "work the room," as Grandpa calls it.) So I walked back in to see with whom he stopped to chat. It was an elderly gentleman and his wife, so I stood by the door and waited. (This, too, is normal procedure when with Jared.) I didn't know the gentleman, but that was no surprise. Jared knows a lot more people than I do – it's that gregarious thing. After Jared caught up with me I asked him who the gentleman was.

He said, "Oh – I don't know his name."

Hmm

"But you knew him, right?"

"No."

Hmm

"Why did you stop and talk to him?"

"Because I saw his hat."

"What about his hat?"

"It said 'War Veteran' on it."

Jared had noticed the hat and deduced that the guy was a war vet, so he wanted to stop by his table and ask him about it. He also wanted to thank him for serving our country. I think that qualifies him not only as having a high SQ, but a high GQ, KQ, CQ, and a whole bunch of other Qs.

What I find absolutely fascinating is that some of those same high Qs are shared by some of Jared's friends who happen to be in the Special Needs Mutual.

For those of you who are not familiar with mutual, it is a youth group in the Church of Jesus Christ of Latter-day Saints that involves 12-17 year old kids. But the *Special Needs* Mutual is different in that it is designed specifically for those who have handicaps. It, too, starts at 12 years of age but can go on until the handicapped member is gray or balding. Those "kids" never seem to lose their being a "kid at heart" status.

Several years ago I was called to be a teacher in that organization. What I noticed about those sweet special kids was that they all had very high ULQs – Unconditional Love Quotients. Evidently, they were of the Mother Teresa set: she said, *"If you judge people, you have no time to love them."* They happened to love everybody! No judgment involved!

I also noticed that like Jared they, too, had lots of other high Qs: CQs – Caring Quotients, KQs – Kindness Quotients, and SGQs – Sincerely Genuine Quotients. It was a mystery to me as to why. Maybe it was because they didn't have high IQs to get in the way. They weren't bogged down with worldly thinking; the thinking that distracts brains and clogs spiritual input. They had room to focus on and develop those other incredibly important Qs. The bottom line is that they cared much more about people than they did about worldly things.

We Special Needs Mutual teachers always looked forward to SNM night. We had a ball. We knew we would always get hugs, high fives, back pats, and huge smiles. I knew that if I had had a bad day, going to SNM would cheer me up. I would always feel so much better after going. There were always enough smiles and genuine hugs to go around. And where else in this universe could I expect to be called "foxy" or "gorgeous" but by my dear SNM friend Ryan (Though the other feminine gendered teachers and leaders got called the same.) But who cared? It still made me/us feel like a million bucks!

It went both ways, however. Those kids loved mutual. Their excitement for going to mutual was akin to a going on a free trip to Disneyland once a week. They were absolutely effervescent upon arrival!

There are so many other fascinating Qs: you have your LQ – Logic Quotient; PQ – Patience Quotient; FBQ – Funny Bone Quotient; BQ – Benevolence Quotient; GPQ – Gorgeous Physique Quotient; and NBQ – Natural Beauty Quotient. And we mustn't forget AQ – Appropriate Quotient. Those with a low AQ would be the ones who always seem to stick either one foot or both feet in their mouth at the most inopportune times. (Actually, I think my AQ is a little low.)

There is one more quotient I'd like to mention: SpQ – Spiritual Quotient. Though only one day old, alone with him in my hospital room, I could sense Jared's enormous SpQ. It has grown right along with him. I can feel it in others who have disabilities as well. It is quite an incredible experience to be in their presence.

Now that I know better, high IQ should never get top billing. There are too many other high Qs that deserve recognition. A very, very important lesson learned.

*"I applied my heart to what I observed
and learned a lesson from what I saw.." Proverbs 24:32*

More of Jared's variegated vocabulary

piña colada   (piñata)

flip a Louie   (flip a U turn)

orthodoxes   (orthotics – his shoe inserts)

evensionally   (eventually)

si-'millier   (similar)

ravenous   (a really bad *old* person)

15

Thanks for Coming, ...But...

*"Good judgment comes from experience,
and a lot of that comes from bad judgment."~ Will Rogers*

Initiative is a good thing: one person stepping up to the plate to make a decision that gets some sort of ball rolling. That's a plus. Then there's Jared's use of initiative. He tends to be a little, well, green in the initiative department.

One of the main components of initiative is taking action. Jared loves taking action. In that respect, he is like the rest of us. Taking action makes him feel like a person of influence, a person in control, a person who is big dawg cool. I get that. Unfortunately, he got it too, after he experienced using it a couple of times. That *feeling good* part has led to an avalanche of initiative that doesn't have a turn-off valve. There are times I take issue with Jared's initiative. The following experience happens to be one of them.

৯৵

When I turned sixty, I noticed that I forgot a lot. At least I think I noticed that. I can't remember if I noticed or if I didn't notice. What was it I was supposed to be noticing? I forget. Anyway, in an effort to stimulate my aging brain I thought I should try something new and challenging. River dancing was totally out of the question; construction certainly wasn't an option; running for governor ...nah; and since I'm more of a Maxine than a Martha Stewart, scheduling grind-your-own-wheat recipe exchange parties would never make it on my to-do list; so I did the next best thing, I rented a cello and started taking lessons.

Why the cello? I just love the way a cello sounds. When I hear the exquisitely deep rich tones that emanate from that beautiful instrument, my mind's eye visualizes an elegant swan, gracefully gliding on a glistening lake: a smooth, velvety, almost sensual sound. But then *I* play it. More or less, every time bow meets string it resembles buckshot scattering a gaggle of geese. There doesn't seem to a swan anywhere near my cello playing.

Then there are those off-color notes. In my defense, however, there is a good reason for those: there are no friggin' frets! A guitar has frets — those little bar-like things on the guitar's neck that guide your fingers into playing the right notes. Cellos don't have frets. No wonder we cello novices have issues. It is next to impossible for us rookies to know where to put our fingers! I'm finding that making a stab at the general vicinity doesn't work so well, at least not without a bajillion hours of practice.

There are times when I practice, however, that a few good notes actually escape. But there are more times when I'm either sharp, flat, or that screechy stuff happens. That bothers me a little. There are others it bothers, too. My inexperience in tonal quality sends Jared's cockatiel into a screeching frenzy. It's no mystery why my husband *suggests* I go behind closed doors when I practice. I'm sure he wishes that when we built our house we had invested in better sound proofing.

Even though there are some goosebump squeaks and enough tonal faux pas to make Yo-Yo Ma run for cover, it doesn't deter me. I just love playing the thing.

Something cool took place a couple of years after I started taking lessons that brightened my cello playing existence. A cute little lady, Sheree, moved in next door. She, too, happened to be somewhat of a beginner at string playing. Her weapon of choice was the violin. While we were talking together one day, ideas started to germinate. Why not play together? It would be kind of like a jam session for novice string playing adult-type people. Technically, I think they are called *chamber groups*. In fact, upon completion of our very first attempt at playing our instruments together in the basement of her father's home (which might very well be where the word "chamber" originated) he made the comment as we walked up the stairs, "Well, from the sound of things it doesn't look like you'll be playing at Carnegie Hall anytime soon." (Obviously he has a good ear.)

We were not to be deterred, however. We were having a good time. Playing together was a lot more fun than playing alone. Then we discovered a totally *aha* phenomenon – when one person plays with another person, it tends to mask one's own musical faux pas. That was frosting on the cake! It made us feel as if we were performing in a real orchestra ...practically ...if you beef up your imagination a little.

Since we were having such a good time, we figured we should let other folks in on our little string playing ensemble. Why not spread the joy? We had the ideal springboard for spreading the news: our church's weekly Relief Society bulletin. It was free.

The day came for the inaugural assemblage of the happy string people. Sheree and I were anxious to find out who would come to that first of hopefully many fun get-togethers. We were both excited to think that with the prospect of adding more musicians – even if it turned out to be only one more person, it would multiply the fun (and cover up more of our own faux pas). There was a little snag, however; she wasn't going to be able to make it to the first meeting. This is where Jared enters the picture and things started to go south.

Prior to the evening's much anticipated event I had some errands to run, so Jared stayed home tidying up the house in preparation for the musical guests as a favor to me. (He's such a willing helper.) While I was gone, Sheree stopped by to drop off her sheet music in case it might be needed by a new member. Since I was not at home, she handed her music to Jared and said these exact words: "I sure hope some people show up tonight." That's when it all started.

It was exactly 7:00 p.m. the doorbell rang for the first time. It was Patty, one of the more virtuoso-type musicians in our ward. In fact, this particular lady happened to be a member of an actual honest-to-goodness orchestra. She not only played the violin, but the harp, the organ, and the piano. Plus, she also sings! She is a very talented lady. I was ecstatic. We would sound fantastic with her expert musical contribution! I excitedly showed her into our den. She and I began chatting about the fun we were going to have.

While I was busy with Patty, Jared was at-the-ready to receive the influx of the rest of the musician menagerie and guide them into the den.

Again, the doorbell rang. Jared answered it and dutifully escorted a married couple to where Patty and I were excitedly chatting. We knew these folks. They were neat people. Although, when they walked in, it struck me as being a little odd that neither of them had an instrument in tow. Actually, as I thought about it, I had never been aware that either of them played an instrument. Nevertheless, they were smiling, crisply dressed, and very cordial.

We were all chatting amicably, but there was an unsettling undercurrent. The no-instrument thing was a little strange. I could sense that Patty was also a little puzzled. I glanced in Jared's direction. He was leaning against the doorjamb with his arms folded ...smiling. That bothered me.

The four of us continued to make an attempt at small talk, but we were all still a little uncomfortable. I did not know why this couple, sweet as they were, was in my house. They, too, seemed a little collectively lost. I sensed they had no inclination to join our group. Clearly there were no instruments in their possession. As each minute passed, things became more awkward with no rationale in sight.

Finally, the wife spoke up and asked, "Well, when is this concert going to start?"

The what?

Jared was still leaning against the doorjamb – still smiling.

I think I stammered, *"Concert?"*

"Well, yes. Jared called us and invited us to the concert you guys are performing tonight," said the wife.

"What?"

I glanced at Jared. His smile broadened.

I felt a little numb. Giving Jared the menacing double-red-eyed glare, I said, *"You invited?"*

"Well," he proudly announced, "you guys said you hoped people showed up, so I thought I'd help a little."

"To *play* with us, Jared. To play *with* us. Not to perform *for.*"

"...Oh."

The proverbial cat was out of the bag. Understanding hit all of us. We were embarrassed. We weren't quite sure what to do next with this unexpected state of affairs. Not a one of us knew what to say. I think the couple witnessed my earlier glare at Jared and they didn't want me to kill him, so the wife broke the ice by graciously asking us to play a little something for them anyway.

Play something? Good grief! Were they kidding? I could hear my squeaks already and I hadn't even picked up my bow! I couldn't say out loud what I was thinking — like, *"Are you out of your minds?"* And we couldn't just tell them, *"Thanks anyway, but would you mind going home."* I had never played with Patty. I had never played with *anyone* except Sheree, ever. We were totally beginning beginners. Patty was an accomplished musician! It was like pitting a girl scout who had just read a first aid pamphlet with an EMT. They wanted *us* to play something anyway? Together? Spontaneously? Unrehearsed? I'm of the *Twinkle, Twinkle Little Star* set and Patty's used to playing things like Handle's *Messiah.* I started sweating, which I know how to do a lot better than playing the cello.

The good news is that things ended reasonably well, considering the circumstances. Though no other musicians showed up, Patty pulled me through a couple of numbers. I think one of them was *Old McDonald.* We had to make an attempt to play at least something to make it somewhat worth the couple's effort for showing up for *the concert.* They even clapped when we finished.

Bless them.

It all happened because Jared's sensitive little heart didn't want me to be disappointed by no one "showing up," so he took *initiative*. He got out the church's ward directory and started calling people. Thank heavens only one couple made the trip.

The pies de résistance came the following Sunday at church when two people at separate times approached me. They both wanted to express their regrets for not being able to attend "the concert." I smiled.

Yes, initiative is usually a good thing. But I'm thinking one must be aware of all the contiguous circumstances *in their entirety* (with maybe a little logic thrown in the mix) before one revs up initiative. I'm not exactly sure how that can be taught, but I'm working on it.

"Happy is the man that findeth wisdom,
and the man that getteth understanding." Proverbs 3:13

Amen.

Jared's Crooked Cliché

"Throwing precautions in the wind."

(throwing caution to the wind)

16

Horses, Spaghetti and Army Tanks

"Friendship is unnecessary, like philosophy, like art... It has no survival value; rather it is one of those things that give value to survival." ~ C. S. Lewis

To this very day, every time we pass a certain steep rocky mountainside, which happens to be close to our dentist's office, Jared sighs and says, "Someday I'm going to climb up there." The compelling lure of mountains seems to be irresistible, not just to Jared, but to our younger son John, and to boys in general. I don't think there is a boy alive who hasn't had wistful thoughts of climbing on or adventuring in the mountains. That is why scouting was invented. Fathers got tired of hearing their sons begging to go camping, climbing, exploring, and making s'mores. So all the neighborhood fathers got together and coerced their nearest willing and trusted neighbor into taking their boys off their hands for a few glorious adventure-filled days in the mountains. Voilà — the invention of scouting.

Though opposite gender I might be, I admit to being a mountain lover myself. I suppose that living in them for five of my childhood years has something to do with it. From seven to twelve years old I spent a lot of time in those majestic edifices, exploring and climbing to my heart's content. It's hard not to when there is a mountain in your front yard, another one in your backyard, and a river in between.

My personal exploration in the mountains was never a trivial thing. It was serious stuff. I was most always centered on trying to find that buried treasure chest that some pirate planted hundreds of years before which I was positive would be found just under the first few layers of oak leaves. I just *knew* it had to be there. It wasn't until I got into my mid-twenties that I realized pirates probably didn't sail the mountains, especially in the Midwest.

Just as those mystifying edifices called to most boys, they also called to Jared and John. The sad irony was that my husband and I were not mountain-type people, nor did we come from mountain-type people. While it was true that I lived on a mountain in my childhood, I had lived *in a house* on a mountain. There is a big difference: no camp fires, sleeping bags, or bug repellants were involved. We had an actual roof over our heads. We had beds with sheets and frilly quilts. We did experience real campfire-type fires in our fireplace, though, but we never roasted marshmallows in it. No, my family never did do the camping thing – ever. Wait, I lied. We drove in a motor home once. That might count for something.

And then there's my husband: his idea of camping includes a Hilton Hotel with a bath mat and a flushing toilet. Maybe that's why Jared and John longed for the great outdoors so much. They hadn't had the experience, and they wanted it – and they certainly weren't going to get it from a mother who hated campfire smoke in her hair and a father who was a Jim Bridger dropout.

It looked as if Jared and John's mountaineering dreams would never come to fruition having camping party-pooper parents such as Lee and myself. But there was a silver lining peeking through that dismal cloud: *scouting*. Hooray for scouting! May I take this opportunity to pay homage to those adorable scout leader men. It is my fervent belief that once a man chooses, of his own free will, to accept that overwhelmingly gargantuan responsibility, he should automatically receive sainthood and an endless supply of Mrs. Cavenaugh's chocolates for the rest of his natural life. Lee and I are forever indebted to them for their courageous benevolence.

However, the more I thought about it, the less enthusiastic I became about putting Jared into a scout troop. Whoever the scout leaders were might be biting off more than they could chew with Jared in their pack. Though he was fairly high functioning socially, the 'lack of logic' and 'lack of common sense' thing was a worry, especially where blazing camp fires, swift rivers, and cliff hiking were concerned. I didn't want to add a bigger burden on the leaders when they already had to corral a bevy of squirrely, manic boys out in a wilderness setting. Then I came to my senses and recognized our ace in the hole: John.

Jared was to John like a magnet was to an army tank. He went wherever John went. He did whatever John did. And most of the time, John was happy with that arrangement. He and Jared were very close and loved being together. So we figured with John in the pack, the scout leader would always have an added pair of eyes looking out for Jared's welfare. That was the clincher: John. *Scouting... here comes Jared!*

Through the years we were very blessed to have marvelous people in the role of scout leaders, from cubs up to earning the big Eagle. And not only were the leaders good, the fellow scouts were good. They liked Jared, and through John's example, they were comfortable around him and helped him when needed. Actually, the "help" ended up going both ways – the 'needing to be needed' thing.

One of Jared's scout leaders, Rick, who not only was our neighbor, he was our dentist and good friend, shared a scouting story with us of an unlikely duo that stuck together all through one of their camping trips.

On Day One of the scouting trip, when the troop reached their mountainous destination, the kids jumped out of the cars and took off in search of bugs and snakes and mountainous dirt. But one boy (whom I will call Derek) took Jared under his wing and didn't leave his side until camp wrap-up. That was a bit of a relief for John, who was usually "in charge" of Jared's wellbeing. Seeing that Jared had an enthusiastic new sidekick allowed John a little freedom from total-Jared-responsibility on that trip.

Derek was a very nice, very good looking kid, but he was a little shy and seemed a bit insecure; one of those kids that had a tough time fitting-in with your normal average squirrely scouting bunch. Noticing Jared, he instantly spotted someone who needed a little extra help and he eagerly jumped right in.

One of the first things Derek did was to take Jared to the rifle range to help him learn to site in and aim a 22 (rifle). They spent a great deal of time trying to hit a variety of targets — gratefully none of which were the other scouts. I'm glad that I was told about the rifle thing *after* the trip. Jared plus a rifle? Two plus two! (Oooo — here come the wrinkles!) Thank heaven above that no ghastly newspaper headlines relating to that trip ever hit the front page. I know because I checked the paper daily. But solely due to Derek's vigilant assistance, Jared was able to earn his rifle merit badge. Derek did the same thing for Jared with the fishing merit badge. Ranger Rick (as we lovingly called our scout leader friend) said that most of the time they could be seen shoulder to shoulder, working together. There were even times when Derek was seen with his arm around Jared, and vice versa. It was a sweet relationship.

Jared hasn't always had positive experiences with scouting-in-the-mountain adventures, however. On one particular excursion, trouble reared its ugly head mere minutes after scout touchdown, and it was mainly due to Jared's soft heart for animals. John wasn't able to attend that particular trip, so Jared went solo.

Every mother notices that when her scout packs for a scout outing, it creates a buildup of adrenaline which escalates with every passing second. Any good scout worth his weight in merit badges almost explodes before tossing his bulging burlap duffle bag into a scout leader's car. With every passing mile as they head for the mountains, frenzied energy builds. It's no surprise that as the troop lands at the camp site, car doors blast open with scouts literally flying out in every direction — that is, except for Jared. Jared has never been known to *fly* anywhere. Do not get the wrong impression. It isn't that he doesn't get just as excited as every other scout does; it's just that his physical speed dial is set on a sort of leisurely languid. It's just his nature. Consequently, Jared was the last scout out of the car.

While the rest of the scouts were in new-camp-site frenzy mode, Jared was contentedly meandering around the area checking out the bushes, trees, and enticing trails. While he was meandering he happened to spot some beautiful horses grazing in a large, fenced pasture. It happened to be a beautiful sunny day. It also happened to be a hot day. Jared started to feel a little parched. He looked at the horses. They might be thirsty, too. So he found a bucket next to a nearby waterspout, filled it with water, opened the gate and headed for the horses. (Here comes that *initiative* thing again.)

Several horse heads bobbed up noticing Jared in their pasture with the bucket. A few meaty beasts began to saunter in his direction. It wasn't long before the rest began to follow, but now they were on a trot. Jared was so pleased with himself that they were heading straight for him and his bucket of nice fresh water. When they started to pick up speed, he started to worry a little bit. A few seconds later they were in full gallop mode heading straight for him.

Jared froze. His knees turned to jelly. I'm sure he figured that those huge beefy critters were going to trample him into mincemeat. To his relief, they zoomed right passed him. They were heading for their real target – the open gate. Yep. They were history. Those big brawny high-priced beasts were now flying to freedom in helter-skelter mode all over that lovely mountainside.

Relief from not being trampled to death changed to immediate panic when Jared now grasped what he had just done. He yelled for help. I wish I could have been a fly on a nearby fencepost to witness firsthand the chaos that ensued when the scout master realized the situation. I was told that he sprinted for the truck with his assistants close behind. They jumped in, and with pebbles and dirt flying from spinning tires, headed for the AWOL horses. Most of that first day at camp was spent in horse round-up mode.

Another unfortunate experience included homemade campsite spaghetti. (It was Ranger Rick's specialty.) As I understand it, after all the facts were in, the five helpings of said spaghetti that Jared downed ended right back up with a lot of moaning and groaning in between. It included much angst and handwringing on the part of Ranger Rick. (This would be one of those huge disadvantages to leading a scout troop.) In Jared's defense, using his skill at regulating portion size didn't compute when the other scouts were having "how much spaghetti can you slurp" contests. Rick was afraid that he would have to make the dreaded emergency phone call for us to pick up our son from camp. But after the first couple of hurls, Jared said he felt better. So did a grateful Ranger Rick.

As Jared got older, he graduated from the regular scout troop and became a member of the Special Needs Mutual scouting program. It happens that their scouting program goes on forever – or at least until the scout becomes too old to carry his own walking stick or push his walker in the dirt. It's a wonderful program, but it was minus John. John not only had earned his Eagle Scout award, but he was now in college. He was no longer interested in the scouting world.

Even though John had long since quit the scouting realm, the men who were called to be scout leaders in the Special Needs program were not only very capable, they were graced with an extra measure of compassion, patience and love for these "kids." They didn't seem to need the extra eyes and hands that John had provided in the past since there were several more leaders in that SNM pack. However, Jared didn't feel quite the same being at scouting camps without John. It turned out that my scouting mountain man, who drooled every time he saw that rocky steep mountainside, the kid who had mountains in his blood, seemed to have them in his blood for only a day, maybe two at most. For the next three years running we received *the* dreaded phone call usually about two days into each trip: Jared was sick. It was most always in the middle of the night. My husband and I would drive up the mountain sleepy-eyed, fetch a very green Jared, and bring him home. Five minutes after hitting home base, he would always be... just fine. *"It's a miracle!"* My twenty-plus year-old macho mountain man had either contracted the nasty homesickness bug, or had five or so helpings of the dinner's main entre.

ঔৎ

I cannot leave the subject of scouting without including the magnificently invigorating trips to the war surplus store. We had a beauty in our area. No scout worth his salt would ever go on a camping trip without first hitting the local war surplus store. It was a fantastic adventure in and of itself, especially if once inside, you actually found your way out again. That was worth a merit badge by itself. The store even had an apropos slogan that read, "We have everything you need, if you can find it." I swear that the building proper made up probably three or four acres, all on one level, of what must have been at least a dozen acres of open lot that housed every throwback thingamajig that was ever invented for or used by the military. The store even had an honest to goodness army tank positioned by the front door that kids could climb into on a warm sunny day and roast to death for five minutes. It was a scout's dream.

The one drawback to the store was that it had only one entrance and one exit for its customers, which were positioned next to each other. The only windows in that huge massive building were located on either side of those two doors. I counted four. That definitely added to our angst during a particularly nasty hail storm.

Just before Jared and I entered the store on that very dark rainy day, things were turning ugly. Rain drops morphed into ice pellets, so I quickly parked the car and we raced toward the shelter of the gigantic building. After we made it safely inside, from the darkness of the dingy day to the huge bright fluorescently lit building, Jared and I instantly forgot about the gloomy, messy weather and began our exhilarating excursion.

We pushed our cart down each aisle gathering odds and ends for his upcoming scouting adventure. It was a riot to watch the animated energy with which he picked out items he figured were absolutely crucial: the can of canned-heat so he could roast his dinner of spam on a stick; an army helmet to gather rain water –

after all, he's got to wash his face somewhere; some new camping boots (called tennis shoes); a treasured metal canteen with a small dent probably incurred from an honest to goodness bullet, and on and on we went. Our course took us deeper and deeper into the dusty recesses of the store.

That's when it happened. Lightening hit nearby shocking the ancient electrical system into a shutdown. We were in total darkness – and I mean, *total!*

The irony was that no war surplus bull horn was used to make the announcement that we must all stay where we were – and I knew darn well there had to be bullhorns in that store *somewhere*. What we heard was a guy shouting through cupped hands for everyone to stay put. We, personally, did not need those instructions. After having roamed through aisle after aisle of old metal army doodads, smelly water-stained army boots, a variety of weirdly pointy objects, voluminous racks of musty woolen army coats and pants that had to have been from WWI, and all the rest of the cracked, tarnished, stained, ripped, riddled, rotten, and moldy merchandise throughout the store, we were not about to move an inch.

It had only been a couple of minutes standing in the cave-like blackness that suddenly, tiny little beams of light flickered around the store, probably coming from the store's dollar flashlights. Then we heard the guy shouting again through cupped hands that help was on the way, but cautioned all customers to stay where they were until they could be rescued. That day our favorite army surplus store received an "F" in my book for emergency preparedness. That kind of irony can't be missed.

Times change, kids grow up, and now that scouting is in the past, at least for Jared, I admit that I miss the trips to that war surplus store. Sometimes I revisit that store for old time's sake and just wander up and down the aisles – but not without my cell phone and trusty pen flashlight tucked in the recesses of my handbag.

"...and, lo, an horror of great darkness fell upon [them]."
Genesis 15:12

Jared tasted my homemade cheesy potatoes.

"Wow! Mom! You outstanded yourself!"

17

Where Eagles Soar

*"There is no better way to thank God for your sight
than by giving a helping hand to someone in the dark."*
~ Helen Keller

There comes at least one time in most of our lives when we sit back at the end of the day and feel like it was one of the best days ever. Where a reflexive smile sweeps over our face so wide it almost hurts. Where we feel we've just experienced divine approval.

Jared calls those moments "heavenly hugs." Our family of four experienced one of those at the end of the following day.

Jared had finally made it through all the required merit badges. Even through the escaped horses, the spaghetti overload, and the scout overnighters cut short by the hurls, he had finally earned his way to the culminating Eagle Scout project.

At that juncture, it is the scout's responsibility to decide what his project will be. Jared is usually a benevolent kid, so we figured his decision might involve doing something in the munificently kind category for someone else. He didn't disappoint us. As my husband and I presented a plethora of ideas, he was quick to pick one in particular: helping a group home for mentally challenged men that happened to be just down the street. Good choice!

We located the phone number and Jared made the call to set up an appointment with the supervisor. My job was to accompany him only as transportation and back-up, in case a thought was not clearly understood or information was not plainly relayed. The Eagle Project must be done as much on his own as possible. Those were the guidelines.

Jared was so psyched. I'm sure he felt exactly the same as every other scout who had ever reached the Eagle project stage: he was just about to explode with anticipation knowing it was totally within reach. After all, we're talking about the big Eagle here!

Lots of adrenalin was pumping through his little body as we pulled up to the plain yellow brick house. It was an older home, a rambler with a basement. The lawn needed a good mowing but was reasonably green, though the bushes and shrubs hadn't seen a trim in eons. The supervisor (we'll call her Jackie) gave us a warm welcome at the front door and cheerfully invited us inside. Jackie steered us toward a rather worn, rather saggy couch in the living room where we sat as she introduced us to the men in residence. There were a total of five.

All of the men were very excited to see us. One exuberant fellow even had a little squealing thing going on in our behalf. Evidently, guests dropping by were a rare occasion. As a matter of fact (and as we later learned) even the families of some of the men rarely came to visit them.

Jackie excused herself to go get the list she had prepared of all the items the men could use, which included their clothe sizes and a special "wish list" each man desired. As we attempted to make conversation with the men, we took in the surrounding décor. It was sparse. There were no pictures on the scuffed gray walls. The coffee table was old and a bit tilted. The carpet was well worn and would have been thrilled to have had a good cleaning. There were two floor lamps that had seen better days, but I'm guessing they worked. And the men's clothing… well, it covered their bodies. Other than that, there was nothing positive to say about their apparel. The place just did not have the word "happy" written anywhere on it.

Jared didn't waste time with his presentation to Jackie and the men, explaining why he was there and what he hoped would be the outcome for them. *(More squealing)* It was difficult not to get their hopes up too high. We had no crystal ball to tell us how benevolent the surrounding neighborhoods were going to be in donating what the men and the home needed. But the intensity with which the men focused on us with those huge expectant smiles on their faces melted our hearts. It was then that we silently committed ourselves to personally add to whatever the donations ended up lacking to make sure the list was complete. These sweet men *would* be happy with the end result. These men *would* get all that they needed and wanted. In addition, we would make sure their surroundings got a good face lift.

There were bittersweet feelings that Jared and I shared upon leaving that home and the company of those men. We were now determined more than ever to make sure the project would be a success. However, after he had initially presented his plan to the men, and after the responsive smiles, claps, and squeals, he began to comprehend the import of his project. He realized just how much this meant to those gentlemen. I think he knew that he would have to work his tail off to make sure it would be a total success. The pressure was on.

I helped him create a flyer with all the information necessary. It took us most of the day. We wanted to make sure that it not only contained the basics of the things needed, but that it would be worded perfectly in order to touch the hearts of those who read it. We even picked a paper color that was "just right" for the flyer. We would not let these men down.

We printed well over a hundred copies. Jared and John delivered every one of them to the surrounding neighborhoods. They were sunburned, sweating, and exhausted when they returned at the end of the day.

Two weeks went by and the pick-up date was finally at hand. Attached to each flyer was a bright orange tag. That tag was to accompany all the donated items which should then be placed on the curb in front of each donator's house.

Jared solicited the help of his dad and brother for the pick-up phase. They were happy to oblige. Lee and John drove off in one direction, Jared and I in the other.

Nothing could have prepared us for the outcome. There were not only bags bulging with clothing, there were appliances, furniture items, TVs, lamps, a microwave, a coffee table and variety of other items sitting on curbs with bright orange tags littering all the neighborhoods. A few folks even contributed monetarily. We were blown away by the outpouring of generosity and the bounty of the contributions. It took all of us, including the solicited help of extended family and friends, the entire day to round up everything. Then it took an additional few days to separate and categorize it all.

By the end of the last day, we were totally worn out, yet so grateful and thrilled by the generosity of people that we could hardly wait to spring the joy to the group home residents with the sheer mountain of gifts.

Jared made the final phone call. He told Jackie that we were ready to deliver the contributions we had gathered. We coached him not to tell her just how much stuff we had. We thought it would be a nice surprise.

As we pulled in the driveway, we could see the men peeking out of the living room window. As soon as they saw the overloaded truck followed by the loaded down cars and vans assaulting the driveway, the door flew open and bodies came flying outside with arms flailing accompanied by jumping, shouting, and cheering, with a few happy tears thrown in the mix. It was an awesome, awesome sight.

Jared leaned over to me and quietly remarked, "It feels like Christmas, Mom."

I wholeheartedly agreed.

Then he added, "You know what?"

"What, sweetie."

"I actually sorta feel like Santa Claus."

Indeed.

Yes, that day was one for the record books as one of the best days ever. Thanks to our little benevolent Jared and his Eagle Scout project, there were enough "heavenly hugs" to go around.

"Therefore, strengthen your brethren in all your conversation, in all your prayers, in all your exhortations, and in all your doings."
DC 108:7

Jared's Crooked Cliché

"I'd better get all my sparrows lined up."

(Get all my ducks in a row)

18

Impromptu

*"…assistance will come to you through the Holy Ghost as
spiritual guidance. It is a power, beyond your own capability,
that a loving Heavenly Father wants you to use consistently…"*
~ Richard G. Scott

For those of you who believe that God touches our lives in miraculous ways, I would like to share an awesome experience with you.

Jared has grown up as a member of the Church of Jesus Christ of Latter-day Saints. As such he has had many opportunities to present talks in front of our members in church during Sacrament meetings, just as all our member children and adults have. It's a very important part of our Sunday growth and experience.

But I learned early on that Jared always needed a script to follow. To allow him an open forum was never a good idea. This was because Jared never got the jitters in front of a congregation. He thoroughly enjoys the limelight. Given the floor, he can speak for hours with no particular subject in mind, aimless verbal wandering, especially during the bearing of his testimony. Part of the reason is that he loves everyone in our ward. (Actually, he loves *every living human being*, regardless of denomination, gender, color, ethnicity, temperament, apparel, or cuisine preference.) Plus, he feels that his love is always genuinely and indubitably reciprocated. Consequently, he is very comfortable "up front" so to speak. However, that started to become a bit of a problem.

I remember how proud I was the first time he stood up in our pew to bear his testimony during Testimony Meeting. As Church members, bearing our testimony is something we individually choose to do usually about two, maybe three times a year. By so doing, it not only strengthens our own testimony, but it strengths others. A beautiful and sacred spirit is always felt when someone bears a heartfelt testimony.

Jared had been sufficiently taught by the scriptures, by his primary teachers, and by us the proper way to bear a testimony, so his background was sound. He began perfectly: he testified that he knew God and Christ lived; that he knew he had a heavenly Father and heavenly Mother who loved him; that he knew the gospel was true; and then he looked around the room at all the members that he loved so dearly, and began to migrate away from the "bearing of testimony" part to the "drifting" part: "...and I love the Saunders, and the Evans, and the Halls, and the bishop, and my primary teacher, and the birds, and the mountains, and spaghetti, and..."

My husband, who was sitting at the far end of the pew (too far away from a grabbing Jared distance), was giving me the evil eye along with dictatorial hand gestures. He wanted me to make him sit down posthaste! I knew what he was really afraid of. He felt like Jared was going to start spilling personal information about our family life to everyone in the room. Lee was so nervous and consequently sweating so profusely he had sweat running down to his belt loops. I held my breath but had a kind of hopeful faith that Jared wouldn't bring up being grounded, parental shouting, or his dad forgetting to pick him up from school that one day.

After the meeting, (actually, the second we got in the car,) we bombarded Jared with testimony bearing appropriateness. All the way home we presented appropriate scenarios repeatedly and then asked him to give us a sample of what he might say next time. He did. It was good.

Next month, at the very next Testimony Meeting (keeping in

mind that for Jared, 30 days was a fairly long time from the last testimony bearing and consequent parental barrage of instruction episode) he stood up, again a fair distance from his dad's arm reach, and bore his testimony a second time: "I know that God lives. I love Jesus Christ. I know my Mother in heaven loves me. I know the gospel is true ...and I love the Swensons, and the Olsons, and the Stowes, and the bread and water, and my new shirt, and..."

This became an every single Testimony Meeting event, which is not necessarily apropos. Two or three times a year would be about average. We had to do something. First, we made it clear *again* what a testimony was, what was appropriate to say, and what was not. Then, we put up parameters: we told him he could only bear his testimony on his birthday and six months later, on his brother's birthday: as in twice a year. That routine set-up would automatically give us a month's notice to adequately prepare him up to the actual day of his next "up front" experience. In so doing, we would be assured that he would have a fresh perspective of what was appropriate to divulge before he stood up to take the microphone. It worked. We are geniuses.

As a matter of fact, that formula is currently his SOP. It still works. However, we usually get a few patronizing looks from the newbies in our ward after Jared announces at the microphone, "Well, since it's my birthday tomorrow, my Mom and Dad finally *let* me bear my testimony." Heads flip in our general vicinity, and *the glare* assaults us from the well meaning, but un-privy newcomers.

Now that Jared is much older and attending Special Needs Mutual, we spend two Sundays a month at other wards who invite the mutual to present the Sacrament Meeting program. The program consists of talks and songs performed by Special Needs members. I don't think anyone in the congregation ever leaves those presentations without smeared mascara and well-used tissues. It's a remarkably touching and significantly spiritual experience.

One crisp December Sunday morning we were on our way to one of those Sacrament Meeting presentations. I was driving with Jared and his sweet friend, Jessica (who also has Down syndrome) who were in the backseat. Christmastime was in the air, so we merrily chatted about Christmas and what their favorite part of it was. They started out with presents (of course), homemade cookies, turkey dinners, and then progressed to the beautiful lights, smells, songs, then culminating with the most important part, celebrating Jesus' birthday. It ended up being a beautiful way to begin a spiritual day in church.

As we walked into the host chapel, we were greeted by Brother Harvey (as he will be known here) who was one of the leaders of the mutual, and who happened to be conducting the program that day. He looked troubled. We were informed that two of the mutual members who were supposed to give talks that day couldn't make it. He asked Jessica if she wouldn't mind bearing her testimony, which she happily agreed to do.   But then he approached Jared and asked him if he wouldn't mind giving a talk. Whoa! Even though Jared has been bearing his testimony now for many years running, and has given many talks – which have all been prepared and rehearsed well in advance – having Jared give a talk without 'a script' in hand would not be in his best interests, nor anyone else's. I quickly set the record straight that Jared didn't have a talk ready but would be happy to bear his testimony. (That was something he had down pat nowadays – no rambling involved.) I left it at that.

I felt all was copasetic as they headed for the stand up front and I took my place in the congregational pews. But once on the stand, and unknown to me, Jared was asked again if he wouldn't mind giving a talk. Jared loves the limelight. No brainer. He agreed!

Back at the pews, I felt comfortable as I settled back in my seat to enjoy another SNM presentation. No matter how many times I have heard the SNM members speak and sing, my heart is still deeply touched every time. There is such a wonderfully strong spirit that attends those sweet kids, as well as the meeting itself!

The meeting began and Brother Harvey announced the program outline. He announced those who would be bearing testimonies, and then I heard the words, "Our speakers today will be Susie Que, John Doe, Jared Cassity and..." *Oh my goodness!*

I was stunned. I felt nauseas. My heart raced. I was in the pews, Jared was up front. There was nothing I could do. I take a bit of pride in the fact that over the years, experience has taught me to accept the inevitable. Besides, killing him in front of the congregation might not go over well. I tightly gripped the arm rest, and I silently prayed that the Spirit would attend him and help him present what the Lord would want him to say.

It was Jared's turn. He walked to the podium. No written talk in hand, no notes. *(Oh boy, here we go.)* He extended a warm greeting to the congregation and wished everyone a Merry Christmas. *(So far, so good)* Then he said he had three questions for them. *(Wow, an attention getter. Good start.)* But the "three questions" had me a little worried. I had never heard the "three questions" thing before. This was a new twist. I gripped the arm rest tighter.

He said, "The first question is, what is your favorite part of Christmas? The second question is, What does Christmas mean to you? And the third question is..." I actually cannot remember what that third question was, but I was amazed! He sounded like a pro up there! He was reeling in the congregation by getting them personally involved. That's a terrific technique. *(Go Jared!)* As his talk evolved, all the normal congregational rustling and restlessness began to settle. Soon, all heads were directed toward the stand. Even the children were watching. They were all listening.

He listed the signs of Christmas and what they meant to him – which was breathtaking. For example, he said that he loved the lights of Christmas because it symbolized the light of Christ, and how brightly it shines. He said how wonderful it was that almost every house on every block had some type of Christmas decoration indicating that people everywhere were all united in expressing the joy of the birth of our Savior. *(Where in the world was he getting this stuff?)*

He was using all the techniques I had ever learned about public speaking and talking in church. He built interest by including a personal story. He included a couple of apt scriptures. He threw in some humor. Never at any time were his thoughts and words disjointed, and there was not one *"and...a"* throughout his entire discourse. It just flowed! It was as if he was reading from a beautifully prepared script. Finally he reviewed, summarized, then concluded by bearing a short but heartfelt testimony of his Heavenly Older Brother and wished Him a happy birthday.

I had not brought a pad or pencil. I fervently wished that I had! I knew that my little brain would never be able to recall the detail necessary to remember all that he said nor be able to preserve the magic of that moment.

This was not the talk of an amateur. This was certainly not the talk of a young man with a mental disability. There was no disability present! It was a talk that would have made any university student majoring in public oration proud. He sounded like an apostle up there at that podium. I could see the looks of surprise and wonder on the faces of the SNM leaders who were on the stand behind him, including the host bishopric. I, myself, picked my own jaw off the floor. We had all just witnessed the spirit speaking through the heart of a special young man who was willing to be an instrument in the hands of God that day. But it wasn't just what we heard, it was what we *felt*. It was spirit teaching spirit. An absolute miracle.

Brother David A. Bednar, an apostle in our church has said, "The power of your testimony does not come from sophisticated language or effective presentation. Rather, it is the result of revelation conveyed by the power of the Holy Ghost."

That day we witnessed a miracle. That day, we were taught by the Lord through one of the Lord's elect.

"Do ye not remember that I said unto you that after ye had received the Holy Ghost ye could speak with the tongue of angels?" 2 Nephi 32:2

Jared's Crooked Cliché

"Cooking two birds in one stove"

(Another attempt at "Killing two birds with one stone.")

19

He Ain't Heavy

"A brother is a friend given by nature." ~ *Jean Baptiste Legouve*

Remember the Marx brothers? Maybe most of you reading this might be too young to know who they were. Actually, they were also before my time, even though I was once informed by Benny, my youngest grandson, that I was older than dirt.

For those of you who don't know, these brothers happened to be a comedic trio. Wait a minute... a foursome. Hold on... were there five? They kept changing. Well, I'll stick with the most famous three: Groucho, Harpo, and Chico.

The television episodes of The Marx Brothers were in black and white. That gives you a big hint at how old the series was. (The 1950s!) But being in black and white didn't deter me in the least. Anytime one of their old episodes was playing, I would be glued to the TV set.

They were hilarious. I love hilarious. Hilarious ranks right up there with the importance of cherry pie alamode and fireworks. In fact, there is a saying that solidifies a huge benefit of hilarious: "You don't stop laughing because you grow old, you grow old because you stop laughing." There you go. We should laugh our heads off as often as possible.

That brings a question to mind: I wonder if laughing also annihilates saggy, wrinkly skin? If that's the case, count me in on the laughter brigade. As a matter of fact, I'm already on my way:

just looking in the mirror when I get up in the morning has me in hysterics.

Those crazy Marx guys were loose cannons, a little nuts, and would do anything for a laugh. That alone was worth the watching. Even if a person weren't into humor, was doggedly deadpan, and totally void of anything resembling a funny bone, I'm certain they couldn't stop themselves from being drawn to a TV screen when one of the Max Brothers episodes was running. And I'd bet my grandfather's rubber chicken that they would end up generating an impressive snicker. The side-splitting mayhem those guys created was impossible to ignore.

Not only were their physical characteristics humorously odd, but even their names were a crack up. There was Harpo – he had wild frizzy red hair. One would think that playing a comedic mute was sort of an oxymoron, until one saw him scuttling around whistling in expressive pantomime while honking an oversized tricycle horn as his method of communication. (Actually, it was a taxi cab horn, but I don't think you young folk can grasp the vision of an automobile having its horn on the *outside* of a car with which the driver had to manually squeeze, so I'll stick with tricycle horn.)

Then there was Groucho – always had a cigar poking out from beneath a thick greasepaint moustache. Instead of a normal walk, he did a sort of creeping bent-kneed glide, like Quasimodo with deviant facial hair. He had a quick wit which morphed into a slurred innuendo-laden chatter. He had a wittily sarcastic remark for nearly everything, everyone, and every occasion.

Chico, to me, looked almost normal, except for his hat – it was sort of like an upside-down ice cream cone with a rim. Oh, and he did have one peculiar quirk: he spoke with a heavy fake Italian accent. He was not Italian. I find that hilarious.

Although each brother was unique (albeit in bizarre ways) they worked and lived as a cohesive team. I think that was the bottom line to their success. That cohesiveness was their secret formula.

In my motherly opinion, the basis for any solid cohesive brotherly team is that same type of harmony – no squabbling, no bickering, no callous teasing. That happens to be a very good description of my two boys. I don't think they ever argued or bickered or callously teased. Well... maybe they might have at one time or another and I just didn't see it. Or... maybe they really did do it, and I just don't remember it (which seems more likely to be the case, since I have the memory of a fruit fly.) Although, I am extremely relieved that they were minus the Marx brothers' goofy part. I can't deal with goofy.

The point being, even though Jared and John were blood brothers, they rarely fought and never teased each other in a mean spirited way. They were best buddies. As a matter of fact, John was one of the most important people in Jared's life. I am firmly convinced that Jared would not be functioning one-tenth his present ability level had it not been for his younger brother, John. John's natural influence and example played an insurmountable role in Jared's development. Jared would watch John do things and hear John say things, and then try to emulate him. We later learned that using this technique was the very best way for a person with mental challenges to learn. We didn't know that, however, when we made *The Plan.*

The Plan: Since Jared was our firstborn, we made a decision to put having another baby on hold until Jared reached at least four years of age. That way we would be able to spend all the time and effort necessary to help him through infanthood as well as toddlerhood, and that way he would hopefully be cruising on foot by that four-year landmark. The powers that be say that those first few years are absolutely crucial to the mental and physical development of a child with a mental disability. With the myriad of teachers, therapists, specialist, nurses and doctors who worked with Jared, and who required that we follow up on their prescribed interventions, we knew we would definitely be tied up for those first few years. Logic screamed to wait at least four years before bringing child number two into existence.

In addition, and just as important, the four year gap would insure that no vital time would be taken away from the needs of child number two. We would be able to give the follow-up kid all the time and attention he, too, would need and deserve.

But just as some of the most well laid plans end up being toast, so did this one. Though this good-grief-I'm-pregnant shocker was not of our intentional doing, it turned out to be the best thing that could have ever happened for Jared. Someone wiser and All Knowing knew better than we two clueless souls what would be in Jared's best interests, as well as in child number two's.

We learned of "the shocker" ten months after Jared was born. I was noticing things. Something was definitely amiss. I was not feeling right; the smell of seasoning salt made me gag, I had the energy of a tortoise, and I felt the need to yell at my husband, the paper boy, and the Schwann man whenever they came near my general vicinity. I took the test. Geez-Louise – I was with child! Saying I was flabbergasted didn't cover it. I so wanted to bury myself in the hole of total denial. This was not part of *The Plan*.

I hadn't fully gotten over the first pregnancy, for heaven's sake! It had nothing to do with my baby having a disability – remember that during my pregnancy I had no clue as to his handicap. No – it had to do with the fact that I hadn't gotten over the *condition* that the first pregnancy brought, physically or mentally! I had not only gained a lot of weight, but had retained copious amounts of water. My fingers were so swollen that I couldn't grasp the handle bars of my bike, let alone ride it.

You might have heard of that "special glow" that is suppose to accompany a woman who is in the motherly way. That certainly wasn't me. In my case, it was more of a "glower." There was absolutely no "glow-*ing*" involved! I resembled a human balloon for seven months in my maternity mu-mus that looked like they were designed by Omar the tent maker. (At the end of my pregnancy, my husband begged me to let him burn them, with extreme prejudice.) I was not ready for another jaunt down pregnancy alley, especially after I had worked so hard just to get some type of recognizable waistline back.

How could this have happened! We were responsible people! We took precautions! But when a Higher Source pulls a fast one, there's not much we mortals can do about it. We found ourselves on the road to duo-childville, which meant when number two child arrived on the scene – our little twosome would span only 18 months apart. Gadzooks! This was going to be the equivalent of having twins, and I cannot multitask. I was anything but prepared for this news. I did not sign up for twins!

Here was one of those major hiccups along the journey called Life that can only be described as just plain nuts. Not only would I have two infant-type people, one would complicate matters do to his disability. And since children with Downs lag behind the average child in physical as well as mental ability, I was picturing myself trying to haul two babies around, one on each hip, or in their little infant carriers – one in each hand, just to get groceries or to run errands. The thought occurred to me that I wouldn't have any hands left to carry said groceries, errand paraphernalia, or even a diaper bag.

And so it was. But let me clarify: it was just nuts for my husband and me, not for the little twosome. They were like Batman and Robin, Lewis and Clark, cops and donuts. They were an inseparable team, and it was very clear that they loved each other very much. As a matter of fact, they were always a little lost when they were without one another.

As I reminisced over those early parenting years, I became concerned. Questions began to surface that I had never thought of before. From my side of the fence, John always seemed happy with life growing up. He seemed well adjusted and didn't show any signs of feeling neglected due to living with a brother with a handicap – a brother who needed a great deal of our time, effort and attention. But that was *my* perception. I began to wonder what it had really been like from John's point of view. Had he ever felt slighted? Encumbered? Ignored? It would have been completely justifiable as I thought back.

I remembered when they were just little guys how complete strangers would notice Jared first, offering him suckers, giving him the irresistible cheeky pinch, tousle his hair, and then as an afterthought, notice John.

John happened to be not only a darling baby with this

gorgeous head of beautiful thick shiny blonde hair and these big beautiful striking blue eyes, but he was also naturally likeable. However, when folks saw Jared and recognized he had a handicap, they became overly attentive to him and didn't even seem to notice little John was there. That could knock anyone's self-esteem down a notch.

Several other questions plagued my brain about how John must have felt by being left in the dust of social attention. So I called John on the phone to get some long overdue questions resolved.

His answers surprised me. To the first question he responded quickly and confidently, and much to my relief, said he had never felt slighted. As a matter of fact, he said he was even grateful that Jared got most of the attention that would have made the shy little guy that he was, uncomfortable.

It would have been impossible not to notice this inequitable one-sided child interest from well-meaning folks. But Lee and I were worried about the fact that it happened *all the time*. We determined to make up for the imbalance-of-attention thing by either finding or creating opportunities for John to receive his own amount of attention and recognition. From John's answers to my questions, apparently that strategy had worked.

I asked him another question: was there ever a specific point in time when he realized there was a difference between him and his brother. Thoughtfully, he responded that he couldn't remember when he noticed a difference. He always knew Jared had Down syndrome, but it didn't seem to alter the way he felt about his brother. He just always knew he wanted to help him and be there for him, he said.

I thought back about the time when John started high school. Before that time, Jared and John had attended different schools in elementary and junior high, but in high school they attended the same school with the same people. Since Jared preceded him by a couple of years I wondered if that made a difference to John.

This time John's answer shocked me a little. He said there was a sort of plus to Jared's being overly-noticed phenomenon. Lots of the kids and teachers knew Jared, and most everyone liked him. So when John got to high school and started meeting people, it wasn't a surprise when more often than not they would say, "Oh, you must be Jared's brother!" John said this smoothed the way a great deal. He felt there was already a connection.

So in the annals of John's high school career, he came to be known as "the brother of Jared." That might seem like a self-esteem breaker. I thought it might have made him feel devalued or even jealous. But it hadn't. He answered by saying he felt proud.

I had another concern that plagued me. I wondered if John ever felt envious that his friends had brothers who didn't have handicaps, brothers who could drive cars and take them places, or help them with their soccer skills, or homework, or give dating tips. He said that thought had never crossed his mind. (This kid is a gem!)

It finally hit me. I hadn't even thought about it until that moment on the phone talking with John. My eyes were finally opened. All these years I had never even noticed this fact: John's love for Jared had always been totally unconditional. He cared for him deeply. He always just wanted to be a good brother. And I also learned through our phone conversation that he never felt Jared was "less than" or "not as good as." Never did he wish things had been different. He loved Jared *just the way he was*. All those years John *served* Jared because he loved him. I had never realized or given credit to John for being such a wonderfully devoted brother. It made all the difference in the world to Jared's resultant success growing up. Jared was (and is) richly blessed.

"...and by love, serve one another." Galatians 5:13

Lee: "We're a strong family. We always need to work together. We're a team."

Jared: "An old man, an old woman, and a kid. What kind of team is that!"

20

Supersonic Sixteen

"There is no chance, no destiny, no fate that can circumvent or hinder or control the firm resolve of a determined soul."
~ Ella Wheeler Wilcox

Jared has always had a good eye for spotting beautiful women. This is not surprising. He is a male. Except that Jared gets extra credit for having that aptitude of noticing lovely ladies since before he could walk or talk. Rest assured this proclivity is not in a weird way. As a matter of fact, it's rather perfunctory – just a matter of good taste. I recognized this early on when his attention became 100% locked in the general direction of any cashier, receptionist, waitress or Avon lady who was at or above a level eight on the Good-looks-o-meter. Speaking was not required. He just enjoyed the view.

With this in mind, my husband and I shouldn't have been so shocked when he entered the dating domain much earlier than we had expected, but the way it happened caught us totally off guard.

As parents we had a firm belief that dating begins at age sixteen and not one minute sooner. It was not only good counsel by our Church, it was just good common sense; at sixteen one has secured a driver's license, one is becoming more responsible and conscientious, and one is learning how to find a job and earn some money (which equals mental stability in my book.) Frankly, I don't ever remember sitting down with our kids and formally explaining this *16 years of age rule*. Somewhere along the line (probably through osmosis) it just oozed into their brains and became a fact of Cassity life.

My husband and I knew that the day would come when we would need to have a discussion with our boys about the whole dating gig. We were dreading it. Just the idea gave us hives on the brain. Enjoyable as it was for ourselves back when, now that we were parents, it was whole different ballgame. Even thinking about our sons dating brought little wiry gray hairs poking through the surface of our scalps.

It is common knowledge that teenagers who embark on the courting journey for the first time experience a whole new world of feelings and sensations and emotions that tend to run rampant — much like a kitten in a catnip factory. We therefore were enormously relieved that our boys weren't quite ready for it — *we thought*. There was no hurry to address the subject — *we thought*. And besides, during Jared's fifteenth year he had never once mentioned dating. It stood to reason: Jared might be turning sixteen chronologically, but mentally he was much younger. We figured we had loads of time. It was probably years away — *we thought*. Boy, were we sucker punched!

I think the idea was partly our fault. We had always felt that recognizing one's own worth was crucial to a happy existence. We made a pact the moment Jared was born that would be our focus. Family and friends jumped on the bandwagon and were a tremendous help in giving Jared those *ooos* and *ahs* and *atta-boys*.

Over the years, by golly, it worked. His self esteem is off-the-charts strong. If you look up self esteem in *The Dictionary of Diane* you'll find Jared's name in the definition. What is very cool is that most people really do like him. Once, he even thought the microwave oven liked him. I am not kidding. One day he came running into our bedroom extremely excited, and in awe said, "Mom! The oven just talked to me!" I thought maybe a runaway basketball had hit him on the head. I guess it showed on my face, so he breathlessly assured me that it was true. He said, "Honest! Right on the front! It said '*Hi*.'" (That happened to be our microwave oven's slang for "*high*")

Early on I was geared up and ready for prejudice to rear its ugly head. I figured sooner or later the staring would come, and probably the teasing and inevitably the cruelty that Jared would face due to his handicap. We were prepared for those situations, though, and prepared Jared as well. We understood that prejudice was usually a result of ignorance. So when a stranger stared at Jared, I had no problem starting a friendly conversation about the syndrome Jared had and made sure it was upbeat and laced with optimism. I always did this with a pleasant smile. As a result, folks usually returned the affability and expressed gratitude for the information. More often than not, it left them with a positive impression of Down syndrome, or at least, of our son.

Jared caught on to this technique, and when he was old enough to converse, he used it himself. He was not afraid to inform others of his condition. I think he actually enjoyed enlightening folks. Plus, he developed a very handsome and friendly smile of his own. He felt very comfortable in his own skin, and it showed.

It wasn't long before the people in our small city became acquainted with Jared and thought of him as one of their own.

Folks would actually go out of their way to strike up a conversation, wave, high-five him, or just out-and-out give him things. One woman (a total stranger) happened to be standing next to him at the concessions counter in a movie theater and handed him a ten dollar bill, just because. Another time, when passing someone at church that he didn't know, Jared complimented him on his beautiful red blazer. The gentleman was so impressed with Jared's social aptitude that he bought one for him. Jared got smiles and handshakes and hugs and treats. Due to all this positiveness, Jared had no trouble believing he was a pretty cool dude.

Then there is the matter of his birthday. Because most people like him and treat him so well, when his birthday rolls around, he figures its importance rates up there with the Fourth of July, Christmas, and the creation of the universe. He assumes that everyone wants to know it is the most important day in his life, and he just knows they want to give him all the congratulatory salutations that go along with this special occasion. If only the rest of us could have such a terrific sense of self worth.

The day he turned that sixteenth corner happened to be on

a school day. He was so excited to get to school to share the grand news. He took special care to dress his best, comb his hair just so …and put on cologne. That should have been our first big clue that something was up.

Later that afternoon after school, he walked through the front door and into our family room with such a forlorn look on his sweet face. I was familiar with that look, and it broke my heart. I sat down by him, put my arm around his shoulders, gave him a good motherly squeeze and said, "What's the matter, honey?" That's when he spilled the beans. Teary eyed, he said, "I don't know what's wrong, Mom. Nobody would go out with me."

Geez-louise – this hit me like a ton of bricks! What the heck had I just heard?

"What do you mean, sweetie? What do you mean by, *go out with you*?"

He said, "Well, you know how I can date now, since I'm sixteen?"

(I'm starting to lose feeling in my face and hands.) I thought brevity would get him to the point quicker; "Yes," I said succinctly, holding my breath.

"Well, I asked lots of girls out today and nobody would go."

I still couldn't breathe. The gears in my head were working at breakneck speed. *Asked out? Lots of girls?* Holy mackerel! I wasn't anywhere near ready for this conversation.

Apparently, and with great expectations, he had been looking forward to this special dating day inauguration for who knows how long, and it had turned out to be a total failure. He was devastated. What could I possibly say that would brighten his crushed world? I was at a loss. I did know one thing, however, that at times like these it always helps to get a little more information.

Once I found my voice, I asked, "Just *who* did you ask out, sweetheart?"

"Well," he said, "most of the cheerleaders," (*Whoa!*) "some of the class officers," (*Geez!*) "and lots of other cute girls." *(Oh my word!)* Like I said, Jared is confident in himself.

A thought flashed into my mind; since we had never

broached the subject of dating, I hadn't thought of the hugely important factor of *who*, which would be a crucial element of his success in this area. He was so eager to get started that he had been asking everyone who looked good to him out on a date.

This is where things got tricky. I wish I would have had some preparation time before this event hit me square between the eyes. How was I going to explain to him, without dashing all his hopes, that the most beautiful, most popular, and in some cases, the smartest girls in the school might be a little out of his league? I was straining my brain trying to come up with the right wording. Then it hit me, so I said, "Jared, when you start thinking about dating, it's very important that you consider choosing girls with whom you have a lot in common and girls with whom you'll feel comfortable. In other words honey, you'll want to choose to date girls that are more **on your level**. That way, you both will enjoy the date so much more."

To my total astonishment he instantly brightened, gave me an enlightened grin, hugged me and said, "Oh, Mom! Then there's not a problem at all!"

That was a shocker response so soon after his forlorn-ness! How could he have changed instantaneously from grief stricken to everything's A-OK? But then he finished....

"There are lots of girls **shorter than me!**"

It took me a minute to absorb the miscommunication, let alone the hilarity of it. But now I had to regroup, reconnoiter, and re-explain the "more on your level" concept.

There were more surprises in store for us as the dating saga advanced. Those experiences were a myriad of fun, interesting, challenging, and sometimes taxing events; and I'm talking about *for Lee and me!* We learned that when a young man that is mentally challenged goes on a date, it significantly upgrades the parental contribution required. It wasn't, "See you later, honey. Have a great time!" We were the transportation, guardians, financiers, interpreters, social advisers, activity consultants, heavy tippers, Dear Abby, and Doctor Phil. It was full-blown involvement – at least for the first several years.

Incidentally, I would like to insert here that the term Jared actually prefers is *mental handicap*. That's the term we usually use. The first time I used the term *mental disability* I thought he was going to come unglued! He was very angry. Jared rarely gets angry, and especially not at something as minor as the use of a wrong word. I was rather puzzled at his reaction. Then he stated firmly, "I DO NOT have a disability, Mom! I have a handicap!" After thinking it through as *he* probably understood it — which is a skill we've developed — I got the picture; the root word in disability is *disable*. To Jared, to *disable* means to make something incapable of functioning or something that's ineffective, like disabling a computer or an alarm system, or removing the car battery cables. I understood. However, he has since gotten used to term. It no longer bothers him.

Though Lee and I experienced major brain drain trying to figure out how best to help our son in the dating arena, we did have one thing in our favor: the word *appropriate*. Early in Jared's toddlerhood he was taught the meaning of that word. We knew that being appropriate in public was crucial to being liked and accepted. It would be key to his success in social situations. Consequently, that term flew off our lips frequently as he grew. And now, the term covered a lot of good-dating ground. For example: being silly and loud in public *was not* appropriate; being a gentleman at all times *was* appropriate; PDA (Public Display of Affection) *was not* appropriate; a brief good-night kiss at the door *was* appropriate (after a certain amount of dating time had been logged in, that is); sticking spaghetti up your nose was not appropriate — ever — period! and so on. The word "appropriate" was magical to Jared's success. He has turned out to be quite the gentleman.

As I said before, we were not prepared for the dating world of our mentally challenged son. After a rough bout of mental gymnastics in relation to date training followed by a severe case of mental angst, Lee ended up tossing that ball into my court. Yet it rarely turned out as a solo effort.

Since it was we moms who usually ended up going on most

of the dates with the kids, the result was a delightful dual effort on the part of *both* moms. We found that when we put our heads together, we came up with some incredible ideas and solutions that best helped our kids. There were countless instances of trial and error laced with wisdom and anxiety, but in the end, we usually did a heck of a job. We ended up being geniuses on many occasions. *(Yes, women actually do rule the world.)*

There were also some superb gifts I received as a direct result of those sessions: I grew immensely, I was able to experience the wonder of dating with my son, and I gained long lasting friendships with some of the most amazing mothers God planted on this earth. It has been remarkable.

All in all, Jared has dated some darling girls, most also having Down syndrome. (By the way, using the "on your level" thing eventually worked, once he understood its correct meaning, and his dating self-esteem shot back up to par.)

But the one thing I am so grateful for is that he *is* dating and he *is* enjoying it, just as any other *normal* young man would. It's something I hadn't even thought about when he was born. If only I would have known this would happen, it would have eased my mind considerably. It would have made me feel that he would be happy and enjoy life, and would be more normal than not, which he is.

Incidentally, I think the whole enjoying-the-opposite-sex thing can be summed up with the following conversation that Jared and I had in our car one day. He and I were listening to one of our favorite Michael Bublé CDs, when he reached for the volume knob, turned down the sound and said, "You know what's one of the greatest pleasures in life, Mom?"

I was a little taken aback by this rather sudden philosophical question, and responded, "What, Jared?"

He said, "Talking to your girlfriend on the telephone."
Sweet.

"...hear the words of a trembling parent..." 2 Nephi 1:14

Jared: "I had a bad dream with a really bad guy in it. He was quite an agruciating character!"

21

King of What?

"The more we serve our fellowmen in appropriate ways,
the more substance there is to our souls."
~ President Spencer W. Kimball

Jared loves to spend money, loves to be *in charge*, loves to socialize, and is pretty darn happy associating with the female gender. There you go – a perfect equation for dating.

Early on, the very nice part of his dating was that the inaugural dates were with girl *friends*. The *friend* component gave my husband and me time to become adequately initiated into this brave new world of his, and bought us little more time to breathe normally (i.e. there was no turbulent hormonal involvement when dating *friends*.)

His first date, the actual second he turned 16 years of age, was with a sweet girl by the name of April, who also has DS. She and Jared were best friends since toddlerhood. She was the one he happened to be dating at the onset of the "wait-till-you-hear-what-happened-to-me-today" news event.

It all started when Jared came home one day from high school in super-hype mode. He could hardly form the words fast enough to announce some incredible news: He had been chosen to be one of the candidates for the king of Harvest Ball.

(*He had been chosen what?*) This didn't compute. When Jared entered high school, we never thought about school dances. Lee and I had been so involved with current challenges regarding parenting and life in general that the dance deal was not even a twinkle in our thought process, let alone think Jared might go to one. Suddenly, he was not only going to one, but was nominated as a royalty-type person to preside over one.

This was so typical of the recurrent phenomenon we were experiencing as parents. As parents, you are faced with a challenge, you gather the facts, you form possible resolutions, you choose the best case scenario, deal with it, and feel a sense of pride at having faced and conquered. But then another new challenge always rears its head before husband and wife can do an adequate knuckle bump. And with Jared, the wonderment never seems to cease. That's what I've learned.

I've also learned something else, only this something else is quite wonderful. To the credit of today's high school kids everywhere, I understand this inclination is now rather common: students nominating one of their high school's special needs students to run for a king or queen of a noteworthy dance. What a magnanimous idea! Though I was totally shocked by the royalty news, I was also very touched.

Thirty years ago when I was in high school we didn't have kids that had mental disabilities in our building. Evidently, they attended special schools elsewhere. Therefore, we didn't have the opportunity or experience of having special needs kids with which to rub shoulders. Consequently, I had no idea this sort of thing took place, nor did I have a clue what it meant or involved.

The Harvest Ball was a dance, I got that part, but the king/queen part threw me, not just because Jared had been nominated, but because of the idea of having a king and queen. Evidently, a royal couple must reign over said dance. I wondered why. I had no previous experience from which to draw. Jared was my first child in high school. So I tried to think back when I was in high school, back when cavemen roamed the earth, but I have no memory of kings or queens ruling a dance. Maybe the idea was just a little too English for my era. Or, maybe there actually were kings and queens – but since I had never been selected to be in the running, I apparently must have subconsciously blanked out that monarchy part.   In fact, I have a clouded memory of dances altogether.

So I called the school to talk with someone in the know. The sweet accommodating secretary patiently described the royalty routine. She set me straight on all the pertinent issues, and to my astonishment informed me that not only had Jared been nominated as a possible candidate early on, but he had since been *voted upon* as one of the finalists by the entire studentbody. *Voted* for! Whoa. And he was a *finalist* no less! Double whoa! I thought he had just signed up.

Jared was always signing up for something. Once he even signed up for F.F.A. (*Future Farmers of America*). We weren't even close to being farmers. I kill house plants. But he hadn't signed up, he was actually voted in by the students as a finalist for this prominent event. What an exceptionally benevolent thing for those students to do.

Though I am not a *knower* when it comes to modern day dances, I am a pretty good *guesser*. Now that I had been informed that Jared was one of the official finalists for Harvest Ball King, I guessed it would probably require that he have a picture ready to be displayed somewhere in the school, and that he show up at the dance. What did I know?

It turned out that I was little off the mark. Evidently this dance was a significantly huge, momentous, big deal. In addition to the picture thing (taken by the most exclusive, experienced, expensive photographer one could find as was the running tradition) and obviously showing up for the dance, he was also required to participate in a traditional, time-honored assembly.

The assembly's purpose was to introduce each contestant by way of a little personal history accompanied by some sort of humorous past experience. During this assembly, various pictures of each contestant in the growing-up phase of life were shown on a large movie screen. Being an obedient and proud mother I put together all the required growing-up photos and paid the gajillion dollars to the photographer for the display picture, then delivered them to the school. He was all set for the upcoming assembly.

I was so touched that the students thought enough of Jared to vote him in as a finalist for king of this prestigious event, but I didn't really think he would win the crown. Those sweet students had shown their kindness and caring, but there happened to be several other rather good looking male hunks from various athletic teams in the running for the same position. Plus, they were all taller than Jared. Tallness counts. I have learned through past experience that if you have height on your side, odds are you are automatically *a-head* of everyone else.

At this juncture, however, winning the title didn't really matter much – that he had been nominated was totally awesomely grand. Winning or no, he was going to love all the attention being a king contestant would offer, not to mention the fact that his self-esteem would get a big shot in the arm.

Yes, this was certainly a terrific thing. But then reality hit when I realized he needed a *date* for this dance. Maybe the reason I had initially, subconsciously repressed the idea of Jared getting into the dance scene was because it would open a whole new can of worms: dances equal dates, dates equal girls, and girls equal a superfluity of scary problematical stuff! I'm not talking of girls in and of themselves. I mean a girl *with* a boy. (More gray hairs and wrinkles, comin' up!)

I was brewing quite an anxious stew for myself until I remembered that Jared could ask sweet, precious April. We had already made huge progress in the *Mom's Dating 101 Instruction Course* with them as a dating couple. She was a sweetheart, she had proven devoted and dependable, and so it seemed she was a readymade date to said ball, and she also happened to be an absolute doll.

I was relieved. Had Jared not been dating April, he would have called Miley Cyrus, Taylor Swift, or the current Miss America to ask if they were available. I am dead serious. That is his typical MO. He's been there, done that! With cute April, we had no worries with the "who." Life would be good.

The time came for the assembly. With battery charged and video camera at the ready, I headed for the school. Good grief! When I arrived, I was stunned by the vast number of students filing into the huge auditorium. It was overflowing with a sea of teenaged bodies, including lots of outsiders as well as a plethora of parents. This monumental event was obviously a big deal. Finding a seat was next to impossible. I wasn't aware of the necessity of having to arrive an hour early in order to find adequate seating. I think I ended up sitting on cement stairs in an aisle.

Once everyone settled in their comfy seats, while I squirmed on cold cement, a hush fell over the massive auditorium theater as the studentbody president called the assembly to order.

The lights dimmed and a spotlight hit the first couple standing at the top of the stairs of the theater-type seating. Romantic music filled the auditorium, and my breath caught. There was my darling son standing so dignified, sharing the spotlight with one of the queen contestants. She was this very tall (in relation to his Down syndrome short), very elegant, raven haired beauty. She slipped her arm through Jared's and he majestically escorted her down the lengthy set of stairs leading to the stage. It was a sight to behold. He looked so distinguished, so handsome, so proud. This whole business was such an awesome opportunity. Bless those students for being such wonderfully caring kids.

The night of the dance finally came. I was dressed and ready to be chaperone for the evening. I helped him put the finishing touches on his hair. (It's a mom thing.) He looked so handsome in his new slacks, tie and sweater. The wrist corsage he had picked out for April was beautiful and ready to be slipped on her delicate wrist.

Here's the thing... on each dating excursion I get to experience a unique and very special opportunity that most parents of teenaged dating children do not usually have. It is another major advantage of being a parent of an individual with special needs. I have the bonus of being the proverbial "fly on the wall." I am privileged to witness every behind-the-scene thing that happens before, during, and after the dating process: the buzz of anticipation during the preparation; the stomach flutters pulling up to the date's house; the pleasure of seeing the shy, yet blissful smiles of the cute couple walking to the car; the tittering of anticipation in the driving-to-the-dance conversation; and as they dreamily glide with each other around the dance floor, I am privileged to witness their aura of pure joy and dreaminess during the dance.

But the moment that will stay forever in my heart was when April took Jared's face in her dainty hands after he was announced Harvest Ball King, and softly said, "I'm so proud of you!"

That moment for me beat out all the cherry pie alamode in the universe.

From this Harvest Ball experience, I learned that there are more than just a few significantly kind and caring people on this planet, including teenagers who are willing to turn something traditional and rather common place into something very unique and very, very special. There is so much benevolence in this world. What a blessing it is to be a witness to so much of it.

"By small means the Lord can bring about great things."
1 Nephi 16:29

After picking Jared up from work at Anytime Fitness.

Me: "How was the gym this morning, Jared?"
Jared: "You should see it, Mom!
        I left it spotted and spam."

(spic and span)

22

The "Weird Thing"

"A true friend reaches for your hand and touches your heart."
~ Author Unknown

First love. What an extraordinary time in a person's life. On the one hand, it is heralded as one of the most powerful and momentous experiences in one's life. On the other hand, it screws up normal bodily functions: it makes one's legs go weak, it make's one's heart feel like a jack hammer, it turns one's brain into a glob of feeble gray goo. I'm referring, here, to the *parents* of the love-struck person.

Everyone knows that parenting comes with some hefty challenges. That's a given. But when you toss in the *love* factor, previous challenges – no matter how daunting, how complex – are a proverbial walk in the park by comparison. The *love* thing is a kicker, especially when your child is mentally challenged.

Case in point: A friend shared the following experience. Her mentally challenged daughter was engaged to a mentally challenged young man. One afternoon, this special couple had a rather heated argument over the phone – which is not all that uncommon for any engaged couple. It happened to be wintertime in Utah – meaning there was snow on the ground, and lots of it. As the argument intensified, Sadie, as we'll call her, lost her cool and slammed the receiver down on her intended. She stomped out the front door, took off her diamond engagement ring and threw it into the middle of the very snow covered yard.

Her mother went into shock. She grabbed Sadie by the shoulders and set her straight by explaining that one just doesn't throw one's engagement ring away just because one is ticked off at one's fiancée. Her mother told her how much the ring had probably cost him, how unfair it was for her to act so childishly, and how sad he would be that she thought so little of something that meant so much to him over something as silly as an argument. Guilt set in. The daughter ran outside, desperately digging in the snow with her bare hands for the ring, to no avail. Now disheartened and teary eyed, she realized there was only one thing left to do: she ran back in the house, picked up the telephone, and dialed 911.

I'd like to share something quite astonishing with you at this point. You will be enlightened and surprised, and it is essential background information when trying to understand the amour arena for those who have a mental disability. I learned this surprising and monumental thing by observing my own son – and it is this: though technically he is considered *mentally handicapped*, I found that his feelings are not! I was blown away by this. What a fascinating dichotomy! His feelings are normal, standard, typical, conventional, average. As a matter of fact, his feelings are the most normal thing about him. In fact, every mentally challenged individual I know seems to have normal functioning feelings.

Let me clarify by giving you an example. Under typical circumstances, teaching just one concept or task to a child who is mentally challenged usually takes patience, effort, time, and a copious amount of repetition. It may take weeks, months, even years for a child to successfully grasp a concept or for him/her to learn a task.

But here's the kicker – so take note: feelings are the exception to that rule! If someone gives this child a look of approval, or of respect, or of admiration – his/her understanding is *immediate,* just as a look of disapproval, impatience, or annoyance is also instantly detected, and consequently (and most importantly) *felt*. Maybe it's because feelings are not something we have to learn. They intrinsically exist. I don't really know. All I know is that paradoxically, for a person who has a mental disability, feelings exist in the *normal* realm. Ergo, the feelings of an individual who is mentally challenged are just as normal as every other Tom, Dick, or Harry's.

This presents a huge gap between "feelings" and "comprehension." In other words, the first-time-falling-in-love event may happen at an age that is nowhere near the knowing-what-the-heck-is-happening-to-me age. This is why most parents feel like a bomb just detonated in their parenting world when feelings of love enter their handicapped child's life.

We were no exception. There was much to investigate, much to extrapolate, much to explain, and a huge amount of expended effort that went into helping our son in the realm of love and everything that went with it.

When we were plunged into this new adventure, it took us by surprise. I say "we" because these types of relationships do not just involve the two little lovebirds. Oh, no. It involves the parents, the entire family, extended family, close friends, teachers, neighbors, etc.

Jared had been in the world of dating for a couple of years up to this point. During this time, my husband and I had been industriously working with him on appropriateness when in the physical vicinity of girls, when actually on a date with a girl, and everything in between. There were occasional backfires, misfires, and unexpected booby traps, but mostly things moved along without too many catastrophes in the appropriateness-in-dating sphere. He was prepared for the next step: *love*.

Jared and I happened to be attending a PALS workshop in Salt Lake City. This workshop involved several PALS groups throughout the state. Jared was a member of the northern group. This was the backdrop for his first major heart throb.

During the workshop, I was sitting on the sideline in observation and noticed this darling petite little girl. She was a strikingly attractive little blonde, very fit, seemed full of personality and exuberance, and she also happened to have Down syndrome.

(A phenomenal find!) From the sidelines, I kept watching Jared to see when he would spot her. Note: I didn't say *if* – I said *when*. I knew my son.

It didn't take him long. The moment he spotted her his eyes grew saucer big. He was instantly immobilized. He just froze in place for the longest time. Then he gave me "the look" and pointed discretely in her direction. I knew his heart was going to be toast.

Until now, the girls who caught his attention did not have any sort of handicap whatsoever. This worried me a little. We felt it important that he develop relationships with those who mirror his level where there would be much in common. While it was true that he had a few terrific girl *friends* who were in the handicapped world, not one of them provoked a serious romantic interest from him. But at this PALS event, the tide was about to turn.

As I watched this young gal perform, and watched Jared's attention in her direction grow, I knew we would have to take some sort of action before the workshop was over or this darling girl would be history – lost forever in a sea of dispersing bodies. So the instant the workshop concluded, I grabbed Jared by the arm and in a frenzied array of coats, purse, props and costumes, took aim toward her and her mother on a dead run.

Our intent was innocent enough. We simply wanted to introduce ourselves before they disappeared forever. We were so focused on this vital mission that we hadn't factored in the vision of complete strangers stampeding toward them, which would scare the living begeebers out of anyone. But in Jared's and my defense, time was of the essence. We did not have that luxury which would have allowed us to think (or obviously act) rationally.

Since we were literally sprinting toward them, starting off on the right foot was a little shaky. The mother cautiously pulled her daughter behind her to shield her from the two crazy people heading in their direction. Once we introduced ourselves, and the mother saw the connection Jared and her daughter were making, she loosened up. Now the shields were down, and it was the beginning of one of his neatest relationships. The biggest drawback was distance: they lived 100 miles apart. This is one of those times where "a huge amount of expended effort" (and let's add a huge amount of fuel usage) comes in.

The telephone became the conduit for them to get to know one another (as well as to jack up our phone bill.) After many lengthy telephone conversations they became well acquainted. And after insightful input from her mother, their first date was arranged. They decided to attend one of her high school's football games which would take place at her end of the 100 mile division.

It was an ideal set-up for a first date – lots of people surrounding them, lots of friends, lots of noise, lots of cheering, and the focus of attention would be on the game. (Mothers are geniuses.) It was a perfect first date for this cute couple.

What was to follow would tickle me pink, and yet, scare me silly.

After the game ended, her mother and I picked up the kids and took them out for a bite to eat. As I remember, we let the cute new couple have a table all to themselves at the restaurant, us moms being at another table within eye and earshot. Jared was shining like a little sunbeam, and she was doing a little glowing of her own. They acted as if they had known each other for years. Though she had a little difficulty articulating her words, communication didn't seem to be an issue whatsoever. There was no question that love was in the air.

We all had a fabulous time.

Before we departed company, another date was set. We waved a hearty goodbye as Jared and I set out on our hour and a half trek home. As we drove away, I began firing questions at Jared, just as any efficient and nosey mother would be duty-bound to do. (In the official Mother's Parenting Book, this is mandatory.)

After the questions were asked and answered, it was obvious that Jared was smitten. I wish you could have seen him. As he spilled the details of this most wonderful night, he had this faraway dreamy look on his face. It was quite wonderful and quite ...*normal*. How utterly marvelous to see that in my son! He told me all about the neat friends they sat with, about the great game, and about how great and nice and beautiful and sweet she was. And then he told me about *the weird thing*. That's when my breath caught in my throat. Weird thing? *(Oh boy!)*

The conversation went something like this:

"So what happened, Jared? What was this *weird thing*?"

"Well, we were just watching the game and having a great time when it happened, and I couldn't make it stop, Mom. It was just... just... *weird!*"

I'm about ready to implode for lack of detail, so I asked again, "Explain *the weird thing*, Jared. Exactly what was it?"

"Well, while we were sitting right next to each other, she took hold of my hand, and held it."

"*That* was the weird thing?"

"No."

(Geez!) "Go on!"

"*The weird thing* happened after she took my hand. We were just sitting there holding hands when all of a sudden my leg started jumping. It kept jumping. I couldn't make it stop, Mom. It was just *weird!*"

I grinned... *(Whew!)*

"Sweetie, don't worry. What happened to you is a very normal reaction to a first-time-hand-holding-episode with the girl of your dreams."

He grinned. He was relieved.

(So was I!)

Jared has had many dates over the years. Some have been fun, others have been okay, some have made my hair curl, but all have paved the way toward Jared gaining experience in the dating domain. And more importantly, he was experiencing what every average, normal, run-of-the-mill guy goes through. To me, it was an absolutely marvelous yet unexpected miracle!

To this day, and a few loves later, he is still dating. Now that I'm in my sixties, I am probably having more fun on these dating excursions than he is. I think he will probably still be dating when I'm 90 years old – and that is way okay by me. What I enjoy the most is watching him be 'the gentleman.' Dating like a regular guy. What a blessing!

My fervent wish would be that I would have been able to foresee these things when the doctor had first entered my recovery room that monumental day and set out on his diatribe of what to expect from my newly born handicapped son. I would have been able to calmly grin at him and tell him not to worry, that life with Jared was going to be just grand.

"...ye have need that one teach you..." Hebrews 5:12

Jared had both arms overloaded with bulging grocery
bags as he walked into the house from the garage.

Me: "Wow! That's quite an armload."
Jared: "Well, like the wise old proverb says,
              'Carry as much as you can.'"

23

The Extraordinary Door

"You know the only people who are always sure about the proper way to raise children? Those who've never had any." ~ Bill Cosby

Most parents, at one time or another, have experienced a parental bomb explosion. It happens without warning. It's not pretty. They don't really kill you, but they do tend to contribute to men's hair falling out and women's hair turning gray, and let's not forget those jacked up heart palpitations.

One of those bombs detonated after Jared took a trip to Washington D.C. (without us). He was twenty-two at the time. The trip included seven other mentally challenged young adults. There were four girls and four boys total. That was a perfect formula for calamity.

Washington D.C. happened to be the host city that year for the National Down Syndrome Congress' annual convention. Those conventions were superbly organized and the kids with Downs who attended always had a blast. There were workshops, dances, entertainment, banquets, tours, visits from Hollywood stars and notable political personalities. And last but definitely not least, a stay in a hotel, which, to our son, is a vacation in and of itself.

Jared wanted to take this trip badly. Besides, his current girlfriend was going (*gulp*). But there was a big glitch: our family's saved "play money" at that time didn't match up to the funds needed for all three of us to fly off to Washington D.C. for four days.

However, our state organization (the Utah Down Syndrome Foundation) volunteered to help with the funding for any of the Utah kids who wanted to go. If he went without us, the money issue would be solved. *Besides*, his girlfriend's mother was going. *Besides*, it would be so much fun. *Besides*!

Jared had never gone on a trip without us before other than scout camp. In the years after our younger son, John, had flown the coop, the title of Three Musketeers described what was left of our little inseparable family. As expected, we were a bit reticent about letting our third Musketeer sever the cord, if only for a few days. The one thing that cut the deal for him was the fact that some of the other parents were tagging along to chaperone, so Lee and I felt somewhat reassured that Jared and the other kids would be in capable, responsible hands. *Besides!*

A wee ounce of anxiety still loomed in the recesses of our minds, which I believe is normal, until the idea of our own alone time started to take root. Jared would be gone for four days. That meant just Lee and me. Together. Alone. One-on-one time. Yep. We would be delighted to sacrifice a bit of angst for his magical trip. He's happy; we're happy – *killing a bunch of birds with a lot of rocks* works for me.

Once he was in D.C., he called two nights out of the four to let us know that he was alive. The other nights he was either too worn out or having too much fun to call home. Though Lee and I absolutely and thoroughly enjoyed our alone time, we missed him terribly. So as the time neared for his return, we were anxious to have him back in our clutches.

As we drove to the airport to retrieve our wanderlust son, we were at the ready with several pointed questions to ask him on the way back home in order to pull trip details out of him. Jared was typically not a man of many words when it came to recapping details. (I think it might be more of a memory thing, though. Evidently, he inherited that from me.) In fact, if you were to ask him how his four day trip went, and he responded with "good," that would be running just about par. We were excited to hear about his trip. We could hardly wait for the time in the car to ask some of those questions and get some feedback.

He looked so happy and sweet when we spotted his vibrant face coming out of the airliner's jetway with his girlfriend by his side. We exchanged hugs, and then more hugs. After picking up his luggage, he said his goodbyes to his girlfriend and her mother and their friends, and we began our trek to the parking lot.

We pulled out of the parking space and were ready to start firing the questions when he suddenly began rattling off the experiences of his Tour-de-Washington on his own volition. We were stunned. It was as if someone had plugged him in. He went on, and on, and on. Lee and I kept glancing at each other wondering whose kid we really picked up. This was not typical for our son. Shoot – we could hardly get a word in edgewise. We did manage to sneak in a few questions between breaths like, "Who roomed with you?"

"The four of us boys were together, and the four girls were in their own room."

(So far, so good.)

Me: "Which chaperone stayed in your room?"

Jared: "None. We got to be by ourselves."

There it was! It hit us square between the eyes – one of those proverbial parenting bombs. Lee and I looked at each other in alarm mode, and then I nervously asked, "Then where were the chaperones?"

Jared: "Oh, they were in a room down at the end of the hall."

Lee: "In a *separate* room? At the *end* of the hall?"

Jared: "Yeah."

Lee and I are in tensing-up mode.

Me: "Did the girls have a chaperone staying with them?"

Jared: "Nope. They got to be alone, too."

I'm feeling nauseous.

Then he said, "Oh! And Mom and Dad! I have to tell you! There was this neatest door! Right in our room!"

Me: "Really?"

Jared: "It was this way cool door that went right into the girls' room!"

Both of us: "Your rooms had a *connecting door?*"

I started hyperventilating and Lee about crashed the car. What had we done to our son! *No Chaperones stayed in the rooms? Chaperones DOWN THE HALL? A room full of girls next door? Connecting doors!* We were laterally speechless. I got enough breath back to squeak out another question, "Did the girls ever use that door to come into your room?"

"Oh, yes! That was what was so neat! They came into our room every night."

I'm about ready to lose consciousness. Lee was turning white. This wasn't just a parental bomb; it was a full-fledged nuclear detonation. Lee grabbed my hand and we held tight as we braced ourselves for rest of the story.

"It was so wonderful! The girls would come through the special door before bedtime. We had our pajamas on every time. Then, we all got around the bed, we knelt down, and we said our prayers together."

Once Lee and I could breathe again, not only relief, but a huge amount of pride filled our hearts. What dear, sweet, wonderful kids! I turned around and looked at Jared. He was just beaming. That event meant so much to him.

Those kids had been taught correct principles and used them when it counted. I will, however, admit to gaining many more gray hairs on the ride home that evening, while Lee lost a few more. That's the way this parenthood gig seems to go. That's what I've learned.

"Train up a child in the way he should go: and when he is old[er]*, he will not depart from it." Proverbs 22:6*

After I returned to the car where Jared had
been patiently waiting for me, he said,

"You won't believe this, but while you
were gone I sang a lively tune!"

24

The Passing

"Sometimes adversity impels a person to greater heights, and sometimes it provides the opportunity for that person to be a blessing in the lives of others." ~ *Norma H. Hill*

Just where is it written that the *parent* must be the *child's* emotional stability? Normally, parents are the ones who are supposed to be experienced, mature, steady, resilient, and reliable – but not today.

❦

We hated to face it, but we could see our little 19 year-old furry family affiliate just couldn't take life anymore. Max couldn't see. He couldn't hear. He could barely walk. A decision had to be made. It was one of the toughest decisions we ever had to make. But we knew he was suffering, and we couldn't let it go on.

Never before did we have to make "the dreaded vet visit." Our friends and relatives shared war stories about their own experiences, but we had been spared the personal particulars of that trip, until now. We were all feeling anxious and very sad.

That afternoon it became clear that Lee and I would have to drive our beloved little dog out to the vet for the last time. That's when my husband threw me a curve. Seems he was experiencing an emotional meltdown. He said he just couldn't do it! *(Coal in the Christmas sock for you, big guy!)* Evidently, the emotional trauma was just too much for him. *Seriously*? This from a tough cop who has seen human death and carnage on the highways, who followed up on a suicidal jump from the top of the university stadium, who was first on the scene at a shooting rampage on campus where wounded bodies littered the floor. Whatever happened to *that* guy!

Prior to this day, my husband had always had emotions of steel. Wait... there was that one time. It was the day he called me at work, which is never a good sign.

He was so choked up he could hardly speak. I was nervously holding the phone listening to my usually stoic husband having difficulty pulling it together. Never had I heard him so emotionally shaken. *What in the world had happened?* Being this upset either meant that one of our kids had a ghastly accident, or that something terrible had happened to our parents, or that his TV remote had been abducted by aliens. Then I heard the word "Gizzy." *(Gizzy?)* Geez! That's our son's gerbil! *(I am seriously not making this up.)* Lee had discovered the lifeless body of the little critter in his cage in our son's room just moments before he called. He was near an emotional breakdown over a gerbil! I kid you not. I almost shot him myself for nearly giving me a heart attack over a dead rodent.

A thought occurred to me: A manly man that gets all choked up over a dog and a gerbil but has yet to shed a visible tear over someone in his own family seems a bit suspicious to me. I wonder if there is something Freudian happening in there somewhere.

Moving on...

What was I going to do? By default it was up to me to make the trip to the vet, and solo no less. I had a real problem with that. I'm of the teary sort where animals are concerned. *(Okay, maybe I'm getting a taste of why Lee backed out.)* How could I drive all the way out to our vet's office dry eyed, by myself, with little Max lying on the seat next to me? If I started to lose the emotional battle on the way, the waterworks would start and the road would become a big blur. Pulling over would be my only option. I had visions of pulling off the road so many times that I might never make it to the vet before closing time. I needed some emotional support. I needed someone who would go with me.

The only other human being in the house was Jared. I felt that burdening him with such an emotionally draining experience was out of the question. What kind of parent would I be if I coerced my dear sweet son into accompanying me solely for the purpose of stabilizing my own emotions? Who was the adult here, anyway!

Not me – at least, not this day. As it turned out, I didn't even have to ask. Jared stoically volunteered to be my right-hand man. He loved Max. He wanted to be there for him, and for me. What a guy!

All the way to the vet's I was amazed at his bravado. There was ne'r a lip quiver. In fact, he gently stroked Max's fur and talked softly to him the entire way. Here was a Jared I never knew existed.

We made it to the animal hospital. Jared wanted to carry Max inside. I carried Max's blanket. I was fine until we hit the entrance door. My throat began to constrict. Suddenly, I could not make words come out of my mouth. It was as if my tongue had lost all its coordination. For the life of me I couldn't make it work.

Jared looked my way to see why I wasn't speaking. There was a little surprise in his glance, and then he stepped in and took over. In full control of the situation, he explained what we needed to the receptionist. She glanced my way. I casually sashayed in back of Jared holding Max's blanky, nodding at his articulated request like a bobblehead. I felt so helpless with my newfound speech impediment. I had a strong urge to suck my thumb.

The kindly receptionist whisked us into a special room. I was brutally embarrassed by the fact that my emotions were so out of control. I kept trying to say something, but all I could do was squeak. I sounded like a parakeet with laryngitis.

Jared turned out to be a rock. He was a rock through it all. I turned out to be Jello.

That day our roles flipped: I slipped into dependent child mode, Jared jumped into responsible adult mode. He took charge and got me through my composure paralysis.

I thought back to when Jared was first born. I never envisioned a day like today, and the young man that he would become. If I had, my initial outlook would have been so very different. There would have been no concern, no fret, no tears – only joy and gratitude.

That day, Jared became my hero – Mr. Fabulous Fortitude, with two capital Fs.

"...and a little child shall lead them." Isaiah 11:6

At an outdoor mall, we stood debating whether to take the escalator or the elevator.

Jared piped up and said, "Let's take the excavator."

25

The Long Shot

"The act of lifting another ennobles us..." ~ *Kevin Hinkley*

I always figured that having a degree in physical education would be to my advantage in life. Most of the time, yes, it has been. But as a parent, one of the most profound lessons I was ever to learn was a result of being a little too selfish minded due to my physically centered background.

Before becoming parents – actually, before marriage, or by golly, even before noticing boys – most young girls dream of being mothers. Why *is* that! Isn't that like putting the cart before the horse? Maybe that's why dolls were invented in the first place: to appease girls until their interest in boys caught up.

But maybe I have it all wrong. Maybe dolls were invented by crafty mothers who knew that if their young daughters didn't have an item to focus on, the focus would end up on boys and the mothers' lives would be a living nightmare way too early in life. Enter "the doll."

Dolls have another important function – they help girls adjust to all the hundreds of doodads that come with legitimate infants: bibs, bonnets, booties, bottles, barrettes, outfits, more outfits, diapers, glitter, more glitter, etc. Those poor dolls are targets for mauling, over dressing, over hugging, over fussing-with, and hair so over fiddled-with that some dolls end up with hair looking like sparse spaghetti. Fortunately, the dolls do not seem to care.

As we grow older, we lose interest in our dolls and pick up our interest in boys, then relationships bud and thoughts of marriage enter the picture. It's then that we begin to think about becoming a genuine mother – whether we want the first child to be a boy or girl, how these children of ours should be raised, and what we want for them in life. In that regard, I was running about average. The closer I got to a *marriageable age,* the more I thought about children and how much I wanted them. I didn't much care about gender – but human would be good. Up until then, I had raised dogs.

One of the things I was resolute about was to make sure my own children would have ample opportunities to be involved in sports, and a wide variety of them. Sports were a love of mine. I wanted that for them. But after Jared was born, I felt I might have to modify my original viewpoint. Actually, there were several areas that needed a little tweaking.

The profound lesson I mentioned earlier came unexpectedly – as most profound lessons do. It came when Jared was still a baby, and I was still adjusting to his condition and what it meant to his development.

One day while driving home from the grocery store I noticed a little boy walking on the sidewalk dressed from head to toe in football gear. He couldn't have been more than eight years old. I swear that his football helmet was bigger than his entire body. I had no idea how he remained upright. He was the cutest sight on two legs. Then a thought occurred to me: Jared would probably never be able to play football. He would never be able to walk proudly in football gear like this little kid did. I didn't even know if he'd have the capability to run and play at all. A lump formed in my throat and my eyes burned as that realization entered my universe. Tears started to roll down my cheeks. The road began to blur so I had to pull the car over to the shoulder. I sat in my car on the side of the road and wept.

Thankfully, it didn't last long. The Lord stepped in to jolt me into clarity of thought. *Wait a minute,* the thought came, *who's to* *say he will ever even <u>want</u> to play football!*

What followed was such an abrupt change of thought that I was stunned. All these years I had thought in terms of what "I" wanted for my child, instead of what "he" may want!

Suddenly I was able to see things so clearly – I had been selfishly thinking he should be interested in what I thought he should be interested in. Geez! Huge wake-up call! Now I understood the only thing that really mattered was what "he" would be interested in, what would make "him" happy in life, and how we could help him achieve it. I can't even begin to describe my relief with this new insight.

Though Lee's and my base goal remained the same – to provide as many opportunities as possible for Jared – our original intent had changed dramatically. And when John entered the picture, it seemed natural to enroll them together in whatever sport or activity was available at the time, and those which they expressed a desire to try. We didn't force participation. They could decide. And most importantly, we didn't worry whether they would be good at the activity or not. If they liked it, great – if they didn't like it, we'd try something else. It was a very liberating plan.

The first sport my little guys ever participated in was T-ball. What a riot! Prior to the start of the very first game, I remember watching the team of little five year old tykes run out onto the field. To them, I think the concept of "team" meant a bunch of kids playing together in the same general vicinity. Little bodies were running every which way on the field doing somersaults, cartwheels, and jumping like kangaroos. When it was time for the game to begin, it took both coaches to reel in the kids and place them in their respective positions. I use the term "positions" loosely since none of them stayed in one particular place for more than a couple of minutes, let alone an entire inning. Sooner or later, they all digressed back to somersaulting, cartwheeling, and kangaroo jumping. Nevertheless, on with the game!

Ironically, Jared happened to be first up to bat for the very first game. A little nervously the little guy walked up to the ball on the T-stand. We puffed out our chests. We were the proud parents. He turned sideways, lifted the bat over his shoulder, took a deep breath and swung. A miss. He swung again. Another miss. After the fifth or sixth swing, wood finally connected with leather and the ball flew off the T stand. He just stood there, shocked. Lee and I jumped up yelling, "Run! Run!" Jared dropped the bat and took off.

We were grateful he remembered to run toward base number one. He was chugging like crazy. He looked like a sprinting midget with his short little legs. But when he hit first base, we were surprised when he didn't stop. He kept right on running, not to second base, but headed straight out left field. When he could run no further due to hitting the backfield fence, he flipped a 180° and froze. You could see the baffled *Now what?* expression. Priceless!

Soccer was the next sport of choice. Unlike the snail-like pace of T-ball, every little team member (on *both* teams mind you) had an intense and thoroughly entrenched focus on that undulating soccer ball – *all at the same time!* Lee and I joked that for the five year old group the game should be called *Amoeba ball:* not a gelatinous mass, but rather one big mass of human five year-olds bodies all moving in the same direction as the ball, one entire unit, arms and legs flailing wildly. No wonder some kids went home with cleat prints on their foreheads.

But just after we enrolled Jared in his third season of soccer, a significant obstacle reared its ugly head. It was during that soccer season that Legg Perthes entered the picture. The doctor's strict orders were that Jared was not to run or jump – which is basically what soccer is. It was devastating news! He had been so hyped to play again that year. Now, with this unexpected diagnosis, it looked like he was in store for major disappointment.

But the soccer coaches knew Jared well, and knew of his earnest desire to participate. Those resolute and clever guys devised an ingenious plan. With this plan, Jared could actually *play* soccer.

It was quite simple: they just invented a new soccer position. Normally you had your goalies, sweepers, defensive midfielders, right and left midfielders, but now there was a *static* fielder. It was a stationary-type position that had an imaginary circular boundary line which he was never to cross. He was to stay within that imaginary circumference until the ball *came to him*, and then he was instructed to kick it as hard as he could in the opposite direction. With that nifty new position, Jared would never even be tempted to run. Though there was never much action in his neck of the woods, the new position served its purpose, and Jared still felt like part of the team.

One day, during the middle of a soccer game, something very incredible happened. As a bit of background, it is important to note that neither of his coaches ever made known to the opposing team's coaches nor players that their team had a handicapped player: i.e. Jared. They didn't want that to be the focus. As far as the other team knew, Jared was just one of the regular rival team members. Admittedly, though, it wasn't too hard to figure out.

As I mentioned earlier, when Jared was holding his position on the field the ball rarely ever made it to him. When it did come his way, it was most always followed by three or four players in hot pursuit, which so intimidated Jared that he usually moved out of the way to let them pass.

One day the ball, driven by a powerful kick, whooshed ahead of the pack and headed directly toward him. The rival team burst into action and sprinted toward the ball's trajectory. It was evident that several of the opponents were going to catch up to it before it ever got to Jared. I so wanted him to have a chance to kick that ball, though it didn't look like that was going to happen. But as I watched, something remarkable took place. The rival players were slowing down! In disbelief I observed them forming a semicircle to within about seven feet of Jared. By golly, they were intentionally allowing him the opportunity to kick that ball! He quickly positioned himself and delivered his best kick. When his foot connected with the ball, the boys parted to allow the trajectory, and Jared's face lit up like the stadium lights at the Rose Bowl in Pasadena. What an extraordinary sight!

What followed was such exuberance that I thought he was going to explode right there on the soccer field. How grateful I was for that selfless display of generosity from those young players that momentous day on a soccer field!

When I witness things such this, it brings to mind a certain poem:

> *I have wept in the night*
> *For the shortness of sight*
> *That to somebody's need made me blind.*
> *But I never have yet*
> *Felt a bit of regret*
> *For being a little too kind!*
> *- C. R. Gibson*

After several years of watching ordinary boys become extraordinary boys by developing patience, compassion and benevolence toward Jared, we ended up taking another chance at normalness and registered him with John in a regular community youth basketball program. It hadn't started out that way, however.

Though my boys were developing a love of sports, basketball was really their sport of choice. They were fast becoming basketball junkies. Much of their time was spent on our driveway dribbling and shooting. John, Jared, and every neighborhood kid available spent hours at our house playing DWB. Signing them up for basketball was a no brainer.

Originally, we intended on signing Jared up for Special Olympics basketball. But he made an adamant request: he wanted to play basketball with his younger brother. There was a fly in that ointment, however: his brother didn't qualify for Special Olympics. So we made the plunge and signed them both up for a regular community league.

In basketball, as well as so many other sports, we once again witnessed the kindness and patience of coaches and kids alike. Jared ended up playing on the same team with John for three years running. The coaches always let Jared play a few minutes in every game. His leg was better, but he still was not supposed to do a lot of running, especially on hard surfaces. So the "few minutes" thing worked out well.

The third year team turned out to be very talented. Most of their games ended in triumph. They were heading for the junior league play-offs. This particular game was the last one of the season.

Though Jared was older than the rest of the team members (they bent the rules a little due to his mental disability,) they were all much faster and much taller than he was. But that didn't seem to intimidate him. When he played, he acted like he was John Stockton out on the floor.

The time came when our home team had a pretty hefty lead, so the coach put Jared in the game close to halftime. Jared happened to be on the midcourt line when a team member passed him the ball. Because Jared wasn't very fast, he knew if he tried to run it in it would be hastily snatched away by one of the bigger, quicker opponents. He also didn't want to pass it. He had played so much DWB and hit so many long shots he was reasonably sure he could make the shot. So at midcourt, he squared to the basket, took aim, and let 'er fly.

It was nothing but net! The rest of the team jumped off the bench shouting and cheering. The coaches were jumping up and down, fist-pumping the air. The crowd stood and was cheering and applauding. It was a remarkable experience.

After the game, he shared with me what it meant to him. He said, "I felt so warm inside, Mom. I felt like a real basketball player. It was so wonderful! I want to always remember today!"

I am here to tell you that that feeling has always stayed with him. It was a moment frozen in time. And once again, it was due to the kindness of one fellow human being, a sweet benevolent kid, who unselfishly passed him a ball.

*"Let us therefore come boldly unto the throne of grace,
...and find grace to help in time of need." Hebrews 4:16*

We had been experiencing a string of very hot, very dry, very uncomfortable days for over a week. During his prayers one evening, after a rather long awaited rain storm, he said,

"...and we thank Thee for this outcast day."

26

Funky Fingers

"Giving birth is little more than a set of muscular contractions granting passage of a child. Then the mother is born."
~ Erma Bombeck

It seemed to be an ordinary day for a rather pregnant temporary-stay-at-home mom. That would be me. I was rotundly round, perversely puffy, and unbelievably uncomfortable! I was so perturbed by my excessively spherical physique that I felt blaming it on extra water weight was a necessity for my peace of mind. Those who say that a woman who is in the motherly way has such a glow about her obviously had never laid eyes on me.

I can't help but notice today's little soon-to-be-moms. They all look so much smaller and so much perkier than I ever remember being. Most of them look so cute in their little form fitting maternity tops. I assume that those tight little tops must be the latest fashion fad. I have issues with that. With most of those tops there is no guess work in distinguishing bellybutton types: innie or outtie. I happen to feel that a blatant display of one's bellybutton while pregnant is sort of ...ucky. Me? I was more of a tent gal myself. In my seventh month I took on the characteristics of a Sumo wrestler. My own maternity tops looked more like boat tarps. *(Okay – I'm jealous. Moving on...)*

At the time, Jared was a little over a year old. He was still not able to crawl as yet, and was content making his little happy noises playing on his blanket on the floor. I was on the couch attempting to fold clothes. I use the word *attempting* because in my seventh month, trying to reach beyond my beach ball belly was not a walk in the park. It took skill. It took resourcefulness. It took Elastic Woman! If my arms would have only been a couple of feet longer and a little more rubbery it would have made life a heck of a lot easier.

That day things seemed to be humming along rather routinely, as in average, typical, standard, ho-hum – that is... until *it* happened. It was so unpredictable, so bizarre, so out of the ordinary that I was literally speechless. It just happened so fast. I think I went into shock. I can't quite remember. It was all a blur. Normally, it would have been classified as a monumental day for a little tyke with Down syndrome, and Jared had finally accomplished it right before my eyes. He sat up! By himself! Major breakthrough day! The clincher was the *way* he did it.

Keep in mind that I was a gymnastics coach (though temporarily out-of-order due to baby John in the burner.) As a coach, it was crucial that I make sure 'my girls' (gymnasts) were in tip-top shape. They had to be quick, light on their feet, tight, strong, and flexible. Those last two items were a tricky combination. It was a challenge to build strength and at the same time gain flexibility. Sometimes one tended to cancel out the other, and vice versa.

The girls religiously worked on flexibility. It was crucial to their routines, especially on floor exercise and balance beam. Flexibility made a gymnast's routines smooth and flowing. One of the flexibility skills we rigorously worked on was mastering the straddle splits (sometimes referred to as the Chinese splits). In addition to being a good way to show their flexibility to the judges, it was also another way to maneuver between bars during their uneven bar routines. But those splits were difficult to attain for the average person. The gym would be filled with moaning and groaning from blue faced girls as they attempted the painfully sustained press in a stride position to work into those splits. Some girls never were able to attain that dexterous skill.

That's why I was so stunned when my little Jared pushed himself off his tummy, split his legs that were behind him, brought them around each side passing *through* the Chinese splits to come to sitting. I remember thinking that his legs were going to fall off!

I chuckled to myself realizing that my girls were going to be major jealous – he had done it so effortlessly! No agony involved. But then another thought occurred to me – that type of thing couldn't be good for the little guy. Jared needed joint support from surrounding muscles or he would walk like a noodle the rest of his life.

This type of extreme flexibility is another common symptom of DS. Along with being double jointed (as it is commonly known) they also lack good muscle tone. We noticed he was loosey-goosey in every joint of his body, even his fingers. He thought it was funny to push his fingers backward far enough to touch his wrist, because every time he did, Mommy and Daddy looked weird.

We knew that eventually this double-jointed-finger-thing was going to be a problem for him. He would need strength in those little fingers in order to have a pincher-type grasp, the grasp he would need for, say, opening a school locker.

Jared's nurses and therapists helped us with hand and finger exercises. As a matter of fact, they developed exercises for everything from his neck to his feet, but that was the problem: they were *exercises*. For a small child, routine exercises were tedious and boring, especially finger exercises. We needed to be creative. We needed to make it fun. Let's sign him up for piano lessons! That will build finger strength! ...but wait, don't we need a piano?

We did not have a piano. But my mother came to the rescue once again. She bought a rather old (as in primeval), rather used (as in *extremely* used) upright piano from an old Pentecostal minister. We painted it pink (long story). We were proud of our funky pink Pentecostal piano. Looks didn't matter. It worked. End of story.

Getting that piano was one of the best things we ever did. We didn't realize that kids with DS loved music so much. That was a delightful bonus. Jared ended up taking piano lessons for 23 years from some very patient, very kind piano teachers (as in *beyond earthly* patient and *beyond earthly* kind). It was one of the things that helped him build self esteem and also excel in social settings.

Piano helped his fingers, while T-ball, soccer, swimming, and basketball helped his all around strength and coordination. Gratefully, the piano thing continued. But once he became too old to be on youth teams, we had to find alternatives. We had him start working out at the local gym. Once again, we are geniuses! Manly men worked out. It was a mannish thing to do. You could tell it was manly by all the grunting and groaning that permeated the gym, and I'm talking about *one guy*. I cannot leave this subject without bringing up *Clanker*. He was a large, beefy guy that was bulging with muscle. He was also a real piece of work.

Clanker was not his real name. I'm a little ashamed to say that it was our little covert nick-name for him. We couldn't help ourselves. When he was at the gym, the entire place knew it. For some reason, his grunting, growling and groaning was so vociferous even the beauty operators next door could tell when he was working out.

In addition, he had this tendency to clank the weights. You're not supposed to clank the weights. Sometimes when he clanked those weights it vibrated the entire gym. Normally we would ignore that kind of thing, but Jared started thinking this guy was cool. Now we're getting into scary territory. We had to deter him from thinking what this guy was doing was acceptable behavior; otherwise Jared would start a little grunting and clanking of his own. So we secretly (innocently, mind you) dubbed him *Clanker*. This was never to be said in his presence of course, but hopefully that term would remind Jared not to overly grunt and not to overly clank. It worked.

One day Jared and I were on our way to the gym. We got out of the car and headed for the gym entrance. From clear across the parking lot, Jared spotted the guy. Loudly and with fervor, Jared raised a friendly hand high in the air and with gusto yelled, "Yo! Clanker, my man!" I ducked behind a parked car. I'm not proud of it. Lesson learned!

"Oh be wise, what can I say more?" *Jacob 6:12*

While kneeling at his bedside during an
evening prayer, he softly said,

"...and Heavenly Father, help us so we can
rest from everything known to man."

27

Peanut Butter Shot Panic

"Experience is a tough teacher:
She tests first and teaches afterward."
~ Author Unknown

That is a very clever saying. Whoever dreamt that up gets an A+. Though *she* is a tough teacher, we would all agree that Experience is a good thing. But here's the rub – there is a flip side. Experience can also be a detriment – at least it was on *this* day.

It happened the afternoon I took my boys to get their first flu shot. Normally, flu shots are not a big deal. Unfortunately, this day they were a horrendously huge deal.

❧

Something most children with DS have in common is a condition known as *immunodeficiency.* In layman terms, it means Jared has a tough time fighting infections. That coupled with his tiny ear canals (also common with DS) meant that as a child Jared experienced lots of ear infections which usually ended up lasting for weeks.

Because he experienced so many, we were advised to have a specialist look at Jared; an ENT. For those of you unfamiliar with that acronym, it stands for Ear, Nose and Throat doctor – but the technical term is, get ready... ottorhinolaryngologist. I am so proud that now I can actually say that without stuttering.

After the doc examined Jared, he presented three options

that would help stave off the constant infections that attacked our son: one was to put miniscule tubes in his ears to allow them to drain effectively, another was to surgically enlarge his ear canals, and the third option was to administer gammaglobulin shots. We ended up doing all three, but Jared's gammaglobulin shot experience was the culprit behind John's world turning upside down on flu shot day.

୨ৼ

There's some technical stuff that needs clarification here, so stay with me. Since Jared's immune system was a slacker, the gammaglobulin shots were designed to give it a boost. But there was an ugly side to those shots. Not only was the name a little creepy, but the shots were not your typical injections. This was because the gammaglobulin material was thick and sort of gooey. As a matter of fact, the medical community dubbed it "the peanut butter shot." That tells a story in itself. The sticky-globby stuff couldn't pass through a thin ouchless needle. The needle had to be menacingly large. Ergo, the shot hurt like a sonofagun! Not only the initial puncture hurt, but the thick material going in hurt.

The worst part of those shots was the fact that Jared had to have them on a regular basis, as in every month. The anticipation alone was a nightmare – for both of us. In my book, this meets the criteria for anticipatory torture.

Jared tried to be brave during those injections, but a kid can only be so brave before the pain hits and the flailing and gnashing of teeth takes over. For this reason I never allowed John to go with us on those peanut-butter-shot trips. That would rate right up there with a form of child abuse. As a matter of fact, I don't think we even told John about them.

For over a year Jared had to deal with taking those injections. As a result, he developed a hefty fear of syringes. Totally understandable.

Skipping ahead a couple of years, we're now at the county health department for the administration of my children's very first flu shot. Jared drew the short straw. For him, being first was a good thing. It would be over quickly. That didn't change the fact that he was still petrified. Early on I had explained to him that this shot was nothing like the peanut butter kind. He wanted to believe me, but he wasn't buying it.

There we three sat, waiting in the torture chamber, which was technically called an exam room. I was doing my best to cajole him using my most soothing motherly voice. That proved pointless. Past experience won over. He *knew* how a shot felt – at least he thought he knew due to his peanut butter shot history. The cajoling was not going well.

In walked the nurse with syringes in hand. Jared's face turned white. There was shear panic in his eyes. I kept cajoling. However, Ms. Nurse Impatient decided not to wait around until Christmas, so she snatched his arm amidst my cajoling and let him have it. Jared was writhing, squirming, and gritting his teeth as if he were being tortured by Genghis Khan.

You need to keep two things in mind here. First, the shot did not hurt. Yet Jared was so deep into his writing, squirming and teeth gritting, he didn't realize how ouchless it really was. Secondly, John was a witness to this whole seizure-like episode.

Jared finally expelled the breath he had been holding when the nurse stepped back and announced, "It's over." Then, she declared in a sort of *I told you so* voice, "Now, see there? That wasn't so bad, was it?"

Jared shook his head.

John was not convinced.

It was now John's turn. He looked the picture of calm courage. I was amazed, especially since he was showing such self control at such a young age. He stoically lifted up his shirt sleeve, turned his head the opposite direction, and stared at the wall. I was impressed with his bravado.

When the nurse stuck the needle in his arm, I waited for him to flinch. Nothing happened. No flinch. She pressed down on the syringe plunger. Still, no reaction. Nothing at all. Not even a blink. She pulled the needle out and said, "All finished." John's head shot around in surprise. He examined the shot site. He glanced at me. He checked out the shot site once again. He looked stunned.

That's when his gaze shot over to Jared, and his expression changed. The eyebrows drew together. His lips pursed. Slowly he stood up, walked over to Jared, doubled up his fist and slugged him dead center in the un-injected arm.

I was shocked! The nurse was shocked! Jared was shocked! As far back as I can remember John had never ever hit Jared. Then John spoke in a rather slow, malevolent tone of voice, and said, "That didn't even hurt! You are a Jerk!"

I suppressed a deep chuckle. Couldn't help it. So did the nurse. Because of Jared's reaction, poor John thought that shot was going to be so agonizingly painful it would send him to Mars. His expertly camouflaged fear and trepidation were for naught. He was major ticked off! I got it. Jared didn't. Jared just sat there holding the punched arm, confused by his brother's actions. I would explain it to him later. At the moment, I just felt it would be wise to bid a quick farewell to Ms. Nurse Impatient and make our exit to the car.

That day, experience was not our friend.

"Happy is the man that findeth wisdom,
and the man that getteth understanding." Proverbs 3:13

Jared's Crooked Cliché

"Fitting all the ties together."

(tying up loose ends)

28

"Give Me My Usual, Please."

*"When I was a kid, if a guy got killed in a western movie,
I always wondered who got his horse."*
~ George Carlin

We happen to be diehard movie buffs. For the last twenty years our family's tradition of choice has been never-fail weekly movie attendance. Some people love camping, some people are diehard sporting event fans, some are hooked on "Dancing with the Stars," others thrive on belly dancing (which, believe it or not, was my own 50-years-old-at-the-time mother's pastime of choice). But as for my little family, our love is movie going. Nobody better mess with movie night.

We've tried other areas of entertainment to diversify. Sometimes we try something for the sake of another family member's interest. Take ballet, for example. Personally, I love ballet. I used to teach ballet. I love going to the ballet. But I have a family of guys. For your average guy, ballet attendance isn't an activity of choice. My boys were a flat out negative on attending anything involving tutus and pink dancing slippers. However, my dear, kind husband offered to take me to the ballet on a couple of occasions – as in *twice*. Never going again was my decision.

It turned out that ballet and Lee were not compatible. During the first performance we attended, he asked where he could find the dancers' names. I told him they were listed in the program he was holding. "No," he said. "I mean, they aren't on the backs of their uniforms, like the Boston Celtics, or the Dallas Cowboys, so how do you know who the heck they are?" (This was not a good sign.)

We tried a second visit to the ballet. About an hour into the performance I looked over at him to see if he was still breathing, and he had this sort of glazed look in his eyes. I don't think he was fully conscious. At that moment he started reflexively rooting around under his seat. I'm pretty sure he was searching for a channel changer. It was then that I decided not to torture him anymore.

But going to the movies happened to be something we all enjoyed doing together.

Attending a movie is almost magical: the second one walks through the theater doors the aroma of popcorn is almost hypnotic, it permeates the psyche causing the nostrils to expand; the sight of those little jalapeños sitting alluringly atop nachos dripping with cheese makes mouths drool; and those fountain drinks seem to be colder, fizzier, and tastier at a movie house. And, of course, you cannot leave the concession stand without purchasing an enormously huge box of candy.

Those candy racks are rigged! Back in the initial concession stand designing stages, there must have been struggling dentists who volunteered to draw up the blueprint resulting in an all glass candy counter. So in order to get one of those lusciously cold fizzy drinks or a bucket of warm buttery popcorn, you must first lean on that all glass counter taking in the myriad of alluringly aligned treats directly below. Oh those sneaky theater folk! Patrons usually end up paying triple the entrance fee just on goodies.

But the *pièce de résistance* of the movie going experience is the unmitigated thrill that occurs upon joining the throng of human bodies filtering into a darkened theater in anticipation of the lights dimming and the speakers booming once the onscreen action commences. Ahhh. There's absolutely nothing like movie night.

A few years ago, when we moved to our little town, we got an unexpected bonus. There was a movie theater just down the street from our new house. Every time we left home or returned, we passed the theater's marquee. The lure was always there. So in addition to our regular weekly family movie night, Jared couldn't resist attending an additional movie day, solo. He has now been so many times that he doesn't even need to place an order at the snack bar anymore. The concessions staff see him coming and fix his order before he ever gets to the counter: a large Diet Coke, an order of nachos, extra cheese drizzled all over the chips, and five (not four, not six) jalapeños on top. There is never a variance.

Once settled, you would think Jared might dig into his warm and tempting pile of nachos the moment derriere meets theater seat. Not so. Jared has a rigid ritual. Immediately digging in is simply not kosher. First, the movie must begin. The movie trailers at the beginning do not count. Jared will sit there holding his tray of chips, even until the cheese grows cold and the chips get soggy. The movie must actually begin before chip enters mouth, and not one second before. That's his movie rule.

Since we have attended so many movies over the years, we have experienced a variety of strange happenings. This now heightens the thrill of attending a movie. We wonder just what odd experience is going to add to our movie night excitement.

On one occasion, we walked through the theater doors just moments before witnessing the movie owner and one of his beefy theater managers tackle an older wiry bearded gentleman, pinning him to the floor. They were literally lying on top of him waiting for the police to arrive. Evidently, the gentleman turned out to be the infamous perpetrator who, for the past several weeks, had been crawling around the darkened theater floors during movies, helping himself to the contents of women's purses. No kidding – slithering on his belly along the dirty sticky yucky theater floors to accomplish his devious malevolent task. I am not making this up.

Then there was *The Railing* incident. My 90 year-old father barely made it through this one unscathed.

My dad decided that he and Jared should have a guys' night out at the movies. Jared and Grandpa loaded up with popcorn, nachos, drinks, and candy at the snack bar and hobbled (as my dad tends to do these days) for the theater entrance. They were, however, a little late for the movie. The trailers had already begun. The theater was now in its darkest state. For unadjusted eyes it was next to impossible to make out objects – like seats, and bodies in seats, let alone for Grandpa's 90 year old visually impaired eyes to make out anything but a black blur. He nervously voiced his concern to Jared. But Jared, feeling totally in charge, told him not to worry, to stay close behind him and he would boldly lead the way.

In this particular theater, a long dimly-lit hallway opened to the front part of the theater, where the humongous picture screen blasted one's eyeballs upon entry. If one made an immediate right turn, one could then mount the stairs which lead to the rest of the stadium type seating.

This particular theater happened to have a very weird railing that separated the first three front rows from the rest of the theater seats. (Its purpose is a complete mystery to me. I think it originally must have been an architectural faux pas that ended up being too costly to fix, so they just left it there.)

Now for some unknown reason, Jared did not make that immediate right turn, which would have been the best option for finding a good seat. He passed up the stairs and pressed straight forward toward the screen. That led the movie duo to the very front row. Jared saw an aisle between the front row seats. Unfortunately, that aisle led them both straight into the weird non-functional railing. It was now blocking their way. In Jared's mind there was an easy fix. He simply set his arm load of goodies on the floor and started climbing over! Grandpa was in shock. Jared, still feeling totally in charge, assertively instructed his 90 year-old relatively-impaired, hands-full-of-snacking-paraphernalia Grandpa to follow him over the rail.

An alert movie-goer noticed the panicked-induced whites of Grandpa's eyes and jumped to his rescue. She kindly guided Grandpa around the railing to a safer seating route – much to his immediate relief.

Jared and Grandpa finally found good seats and all ended

with ne'r a sprained ankle or broken neck. We will all be forever grateful to that alert movie-goer's quick action.

Then there was the *Lost Jared* incident. At the time, Jared was 33. My two grandkids had accompanied their uncle Jared and me, Nana, to see *Shrek* for the fourth or fifth time. I'm not sure. I've lost track. This time, however, was quite *special*: *Shrek* was now in 3-D. Big cool deal. We were all totally psyched.

The movie theater we were attending was not the user-friendly one in our neck of the woods. It was a mammoth movie theater located several miles south of our rural little town. This huge theater house was composed of 13 individual theaters. Out of the 13, four were showing the *Shrek* movie. That, alone, was a recipe for trouble.

The problem all started because we were late. We were hurrying. Everyone and their dog knows all the clichés about *hurrying: The hurrier I go, the behinder I get; Haste makes waste;* etc. But good ol' Nana forgot all that good clichéd advice. *Hurry* won over.

We raced to buy our tickets then literally sprinted to the snack bar, which was now totally devoid of customers: the other patrons were already settled in their assigned seats munching on warm buttery popcorn.

Seeing the void of movie-goers made me even more anxious. Anxiety won over cool common sense. I felt the urgent need to get into that movie posthaste or we'd probably miss something crucial, probably one of our favorite parts that we'd seen four or five times, and heaven forbid that we miss one single segment. But things were about to become even more frantic. Since my grandchildren were seven and nine, making a *quick* decision of goodies just isn't in the cards. I knew that if I didn't hustle them along we could be stuck at the snack bar until next January. More superfluous anxiety set in.

My concentration was so focused on helping Preston and Ben make haste that I wasn't paying attention to Jared. It wasn't until we had our arms loaded with snacks and pop and 3-D glasses that I noticed that he was at the far end of the counter ...empty handed.

I raced over to check on the delay. He informed me that his 'special order' of *Nachos Supreme* wasn't quite ready yet. *"You placed an order?!"* This wasn't your usual nacho chips with cheese on top; this was a mammoth pile of chips with everything under a Mexicana sun added to the heap. Evidently, it took a while to build. The little concession person, with an air of apology, said it would still be a while before Jared's order was ready.

I made a rushed decision. (That was "The Big Mistake.") Normally I would have waited for Jared, but my brain was in harried-malfunction mode. So instead of the prudent choice of waiting for him, I told Jared that I'd go on ahead to get the grandkids situated in their movie seats and he could join us when he had his mountainous nacho order in hand. *After all*, he should have no trouble finding us. *After all*, we had seat assignments. *After all*, there was a ticket-taker to direct him to the right theater. *...After all*.

To cut a long story short, *I* went in the wrong theater with the grandkids in tow. If you'll remember, my brain was in frenzied rush mode. I wish I could blame it on the ticket-taker, the custodian, or maybe the wicked witch from the Wizard of Oz, but this screw-up was totally on my shoulders. The sad part was that my grandkids were so confident that Nana would lead them to the right movie entrance that they weren't paying attention to the theater number either. (They have since learned better.)

The grandkids and I quietly maneuvered into the darkened theater, hunching over as best we could to not block anyone's view of the already-in-progress movie. I tried to locate our miniscule seat numbers in the dark – which was not a walk in the park by the way, especially trying to juggle popcorn, drinks, 3-D glasses, and candy in hunched-over mode. But I finally found our assigned seats. I hustled the kids into their theater chairs with their little arms filled to capacity with all our movie essentials. I then attempted to dislodge their 3-D gasses from the cellophane, child-proof packaging in total darkness. This was not an easy feat, but persistence (and sharp teeth) won the day.

With kids now quietly in their seats, glasses on their noses, drinks in drink holders and snacks in their laps, I flopped back in my own seat with a huge sigh of relief. After a few deep breaths, my pulse rate returned to normal. Harried mode – over.

It was after I tossed the first handful of popcorn into my mouth that I noticed something was wrong. Wasn't this the part in the show just before the finale? Was this the *end* of the movie? It hit me... we were in the wrong theater!

Out of relief mode and back into panic mode, I hurriedly packed up all the goodies, drinks, glasses and kids and out of the theater we flew: grandchildren obediently following in my wake. We ran to check the concessions stand – Jared wasn't there. We began searching through every theater (as best we could in the dark). We looked in every restroom. We even looked outside the building perimeter, but he was nowhere to be found. How could he have gotten lost from the snack bar to the theater seat? (What am I saying? *I* got lost!) Internally, I was panicking. Externally, Nana was a show of total solid control, this for the sake of the grandchildren.

I knew I needed more help because the three of us just didn't seem to be able to locate Jared. I enlisted the help of the kind theater manager, a few of the concessioners, the custodian, the parking garage security guy, and anybody else who I could talk into joining my little search party. But we still came up empty handed. The hunt ensued for an hour and a half. I had the entire movie house in a frenzy.

I was exhausted and now extremely upset. Every scary scenario in the book was accosting my thoughts, which was now turning me into hysterical panic mode. I was losing my "totally in control" façade. I could see the growing concern in my grandchildren's eyes. Where in the world was Jared? Did he decide to take a bus to Vegas? What?

After about an hour and a half of searching the entire movie house, the movie my grandchildren and I were *supposed* to be in, ended. People were beginning to file out of the theater. There, among the throng, moseyed Jared.

Had he been in *that* theater the whole time? Why hadn't we been able to find him when we looked in every theater at least three times, you ask? That day he had on a black tee-shirt. He had unintentionally worn an outfit that blended nicely into the dark theater atmosphere. Batman would have been proud. In addition, he hadn't been sitting in his assigned seat. He had totally forgotten about having a seat number. (He wasn't accustomed to seat numbers in our own neighborhood theater.) Hence, after he couldn't spot us in the dark theater, he just decided to find an empty seat at the top back row in the middle, plunk down, and enjoy the show. Not even Superman's superhuman vision would have helped us spot him clear up there in the top row in the dark.

Huge lesson learned... never do anything harried. It causes brain freeze, resulting in brain malfunction. Plus you end up missing an entire paid-for movie. So do your grandchildren.

I think this experience has a crucial lesson for us all. This harried brain freeze phenomenon is real and unfortunately, quite common. I have been witness to it time and time again during my teaching years, especially in places like the computer lab.

It would happen when students were busily engaged in a typing project and oblivious to time. The computer lab would be quietly humming with only the sound of computer keys ticking away. Then the bell would ring! Everyone would jump a foot off their chairs. The bell for class change in the quietude of the lab is the equivalent of a fire alarm blasting the eardrums, especially when one is so totally absorbed in concentration and oblivious to time. Brain freeze sat in: students' brains malfunctioned right and left; computers glitched all over the place; students' eyes were frozen in panic; fumbled books, papers and pencils were dropped on the floor; on-screen documents were lost.

For some weird reason, intense concentration interrupted by the noise of a blasting bell "froze" rational thinking. The "brain freeze" syndrome makes normal thinking totally impossible. Pressing something like the "Save" icon that students have routinely done a million times just doesn't seem to register when rushing. A score of other weird things began happening all over the room, all because of *hurrying*. Ironically, *hurrying* not only put everyone behind, but created additional troubles. Students always ended up being late for their next class. Happened every time. Good lesson to learn.

The other lesson I learned during the *Lost Jared* episode was that Jared was the only one with the presence of mind to walk into the correct theater. I believe that is because he was not in harried mode. Actually, never in his life has he ever been in harried mode. Evidently, he is lacking the "harried" gene. I believe that is a good thing, though. Bad things happen during "harried." I have since learned from his "non-harried" example. I am much happier nowadays, have less stress, and am in trouble less often.

All in all, we Cassitys love our family movie tradition. It has provided many years of great family entertainment, from catching thieves to climbing railings to attempting to fit into jeans after gaining twenty pounds from the recurrent consumption of candy in mammoth containers, enormous buckets of buttered popcorn, and gigantic cups of ice cold fountain soda pop.

And we're still going...

"Wherefore, do not spend money for that which is of no worth, nor your labor for that which cannot satisfy."
~ 2 Nephi 9:51

Jared's Crooked Cliché

"You'll just have to lay your foot around!"

(put your foot down)

29

The Bad Day

*"I've learned that you can tell a lot about a person by the way
he/she handles these three things:
a rainy day, lost luggage, and tangled Christmas tree lights."*
~ Maya Angelou

Bad days. Everybody has them. This fact did nothing to comfort me during my own. It was not one of those bad days that originated as a result of one bad event. No. It was one of those bad days where you get run over by a bicycle, then a scooter, then a car, then a motor home, then a garbage truck – to use a few metaphors. As my bad day evolved, it was clear that I would not pass Maya Angelou's character test. Though I have learned to dance in the rain, and have learned losing any material thing (such as luggage) is not life altering, I guarantee that if I would have had to deal with tangled Christmas tree lights, I would have ripped them to shreds.

After my bad day I came to a conclusion: Satan must be involved in Bad Day experiences, especially the multifaceted ones. I can visualize him with his minions in an intensely focused competition, each trying to outdo the other, and we are their targets. I think knee-slapping, laughing hysterically, wagers, and drinking beer is involved.

∽∾

Up to this point in my writing, hopefully you have come to the conclusion that I view parenting my son as a marvelous, joy-filled journey. It has taught me more than I ever thought I could learn from a child. It is a gift. That said, it is not a cake walk, either.

From the time that Jared was just an infant, I found myself unintentionally scrutinizing other parents who had children with handicaps. My suppositions would usually go something like this: Look at those parents, they are so patient, so kind; and those two, they seem so humble, yet so capable; those other two have an air of such wisdom; look at that marvelous couple over there, who did not ask for this challenge, yet they seem to be facing it with such dignity, such serenity. I was in awe of all of these special parents. What I want you to know is that my vision was clouded. All those other parents – their entire picture was not visible at a glance. Most of us (including *them*) are normal and vulnerable and eventually succumb to an occasional breakdown of some kind (which is totally inevitable. If not, they are not of the human species.)

So, dear folks, this is me. This chapter opens me up and exposes me to the bare bones. I have certain character flaws: I am imperfect, impatient, and a little inanely insane. And bad days tend to amplify these imperfections.

The precursor to my Bad Day happened at an event a few days earlier. We were attending a church-sponsored family Christmas party. One of the delightful perks to these events is that we adults finally have an opportunity to have meaningful conversations with each other. That is unless parents have multiple children, then interacting becomes so intermittent that adults are lucky to spit out one full sentence before one kid drops his full plate of food, another plants her entire face in the desserts' whipped cream, another is in fire-engine screaming mode, and another is playing musical spoons on his younger sister's. However, the people on our ward planning committee are geniuses. Available to the kids that night were cute little gingerbread house kits for them to assemble *at the dinner tables.* Outstanding! Those little kits kept the kids happy and occupied while the adults got to chat. Total genius! (By the way, "gingerbread kit" is a misnomer. These particular kits were not the real McCoy. They happen to be our ward's economical adaptation: a "graham crackers and marshmallows" version.) Nevertheless, genuine gingerbread or no, Jared couldn't have cared less. He was eager to put one of those things together.

Holy-moly, what a mess! We had frosting up to our elbows with white sugary residue spotting our festive Christmas attire. But by darn, we finally got 'er built. It was a beauty ...until we stood up to go home. It toppled before we could make it into the hallway. I could see that Jared was upset. So being a good mom I promised him I would help him repair it when we got home.

It was late when we walked through our door. I was tired. I'm old. That didn't stop Jared from trying to coax me into not hitting the sheets until we could "please, please, please" put his house back together. (For a little tyke, a parent might have given in. Jared is 34 years old. I'm in my sixties and need sleep more than food. He could wait a few hours.) I promised him we would reassemble the thing in the morning.

Well, you know how *that* goes – late getting up, hit the gym for a workout, hurry and eat breakfast, got to do this or that before this or that, and the little edible house still was not getting repaired. I honestly was having trouble finding a unit of time that we could simultaneously dedicate to the refurbishing. (Remember – we're in the middle of the Christmas season here.)

A couple of days later I happened to be at the grocery store. (Yes, it has now been two full days since the toppling and the gingerbread house is still sitting in a sad little heap on our kitchen counter). I passed by a display of honest to goodness gingerbread house kits. These were the real deal. They were darling things! It was at that moment that a thought occurred to me: Wouldn't it be a lot more fun helping Jared put one of those cute houses together rather than rebuilding the cracker one with the yellow coconut straw and marshmallow sheep with no heads? I bought it for $12.99.

Jared was ecstatic! I looked carefully at the package front. It was apparent that a concerted effort, a concerted amount of time, and concerted patience would be required to complete the project, yet I was so intrigued by its cuteness. I promised myself I would devote the entire morning to help Jared build the thing. We tossed out the graham cracker one and vowed we would start building the fancy one first thing in the morning. I was actually looking forward to it.

Thus begins the morning of the Bad Day.

First thing that morning we were so excited about the project that we didn't want to waste a single minute by getting dressed, so we stayed in our PJs, opened the kit and laid everything out on the kitchen counter. Wow. There certainly were a lot of parts. That did not deter us. We dove right in with holiday enthusiasm. All through the assembly we sang Christmas songs along with the Christmas CD I had playing in the kitchen. Those songs were remarkably soothing to me as pieces were dropped, gumdrops turned up missing, and frosting kept squishing out the top of the kit's cheap little frosting applier gizmo. Jared just could not seem to squeeze the frosting out and pinch the end shut simultaneously. But no matter, we were having fun, especially since there were no time constraints.

As time marched on, we reached the part of construction where numerous little multicolored candy beads were to be placed on the frosted roof of our little edible house. This procedure would take a truck load of fine motor coordination. Among the list of Jared's strengths you will not find *fine motor skills*. His short, stubby little fingers made it difficult to pick up those tiny little evading candy beads between finger and thumb, let alone having to place them on dots of frosting on the gingerbread house roof. This would take time and fortitude, but he was determined to complete it by himself. So I made myself scarce, but stayed within eye-shot so I could jump in if frustration looked forthcoming.

While he kept trying to manipulate those little round candies, I decided to stay busy by practicing my cello which was just a few feet away. I pulled up my chair next to our Christmas tree and picked up my cello. As I reached down to get my tuner, I spotted something wet by one of the presents under the tree. I lifted the present up and to my horror found a puddle underneath.

Evidently, I had been so engrossed in maintaining a perpetual patience level that morning as I helped Jared in the kitchen, I had forgotten that we had a dog. Poor little Cooper had been ignored the entire morning. And, well, when a dog's gotta go and there happens to be a tree in the living room, it's a no brainer. To Cooper, that tree was a prayer answered.

I was beyond horrified – not that the present was soaked in urine, but that our brand new beautiful and fairly pricy laminate wood flooring had a pool of pee puddling on it for who knows how long. We had been instructed after the floor installation never to leave any amount of moisture on it for any length of time or it would warp. I could see the edges of the laminate section curling up right before my very eyes!

Even that would not have been so upsetting if not for the fact that I married an fanatic-paranoid type person with anxiety issues. My husband would have a coronary on the spot. In addition, he would become subconsciously fixated on letting Cooper out on an hourly basis so this disaster would never happen ever again. Life as we knew it would never be the same!

Okay, I might be overdramatizing a little, but I want you to understand what this incident did to my immediate wellbeing. I came unglued! I moved like lightening to try to clean it up before the laminate continued curling up like a frightened armadillo. Understand that I do not usually keep things from my husband. We have a wonderfully sound marriage that is based on respect and honesty. However, there are certain times that sanity takes precedence over forthrightness. I was going to keep my little mouth shut.

Back in the kitchen to Jared and the gingerbread house...

As the last bead of candy was applied, and as my heart rate finally returned to normal now that every evidence of the pee incident had been erased, I noticed how cute Jared's edible project had turned out. The best part was that Jared had had so much fun. He was so proud of it. Once again, I am a genius.

Rallying in the totals, it took us over four hours, took more frosting than was included in the kit, and took more patience than

Job – but we finished it up just in time for Jared to get ready for work.

Knowing time was now of the essence, I told Jared to go ahead and shower before me. (This is definitive proof that I can be a benevolent parent.) I did this knowing full well that he would use every drop of hot water in the house. It's just a normal occurrence regarding Jared's showers. So I sacrificed my own shower and spent the time cleaning up frosting from floor, countertops, cupboards, my forearms and knee caps.

Jared, now showered and clean and ready for work, made his appearance just as I finished picking up the last of the many tiny round gingerbread kit candies that were happily rolling around the kitchen floor. I was still a mess and not even dressed, but no matter. I threw a coat over my pajamas, and with my trusty faded red bandana covering my dirty hair, we headed for the car. As we backed out of the garage, Jared asked, "Would you mind if we go to Maverick to get me a drink for work first?" (It is just down the highway about a mile.)

"Not a problem." After all, I planned to stay in the car.

"Thanks." *(Pause)* "And while we're at it, could we cash my paycheck at the bank?" (Another two miles in the opposite direction.) "Then, maybe, if it's not too much trouble, stop off at Burger King on the way so I can get a chicken sandwich to take to work for lunch?" (He is king of the smooth talkers.)

I hesitated only slightly. After all, it really wasn't a big deal time wise. Like I said, there was nothing pressing that day, plus I wouldn't have to get out of the car, plus I was covered from the waist up by my coat. Anyone who looked into my car window would never be the wiser that I was in sleepwear. I was willing to take the risk.

Cooper and I were waiting patiently at our first stop in Maverick's busy parking lot for Jared to return to the car with his mountainous 44 ounce fountain drink. As I waited, I happened to peek through the steering wheel to glance at the outside temperature gauge: 19 degrees. It was one of our colder winter mornings. Then I noticed, next to the temperature gauge, the tire indicator light was glowing orange. I felt alarm rear its ugly head, then remembered that our little tire indicator light was extremely sensitive. It could be set off by the slightest change in tire pressure, like on really cold or really hot days. That light hardly ever indicated an actual flat tire. No worries.

As Jared approached our car, I rolled down my window, stuck my head out and asked him to take a quick peek at all the tires to see if one looked just a little lower than the others. I, myself, wasn't about to get out of the car in my pajamas to check tires.

He announced, "Yep! We got a flat one, Mom. Flatter than a pancake!"

When he got in the car, reality hit: I'm sitting in a car at Maverick in my pajamas. I am wearing a faded old red bandana over my head, and slippers. I am totally void of make-up. Jared and Cooper are staring at me, waiting for my declaration of how I am going to save the day. I have a pancake for a tire. I am doomed!

I promised myself I would not panic, yet I felt myself begin to hyperventilate. Now what? Lee was at a workshop 100 miles away. He would be gone the entire day. I figured I'd call him anyway to hear his calming voice and ask his advice. He didn't answer his cell. Dang his hide! His voicemail kicked in, so I left a message. I squeezed the phone, involuntarily shook it a little, contemplated tossing it out the window, and proceeded to break out in a cold sweat.

Let me make clear that I am not a flat tire person. Tire stuff is my husband's forte, not mine. Years ago I had a flat tire once. However, two sweet men in a pick-up truck behind me saw it blow, followed me off the road, and promptly changed it for me. That was when I was much younger and much prettier and there were no wrinkles or sagging skin on my person. It doesn't work that way now that I'm in my sixties and in flannel pajamas.

With no flat-tire-changing experience in my personal history, my little brain was going ninety per when I notice an air pump machine across the parking lot. The thought occurred to me that if I could put some air in the tire, I might be able to get to the Big O

Tire establishment a couple of miles down the road before it went flat again. What a relief – not only that I had a plan, but that it might work. I might not be stranded after all.

As we slowly, carefully drove over to the air pump, I had to engage in a little verbal manipulation to get Jared to realize that our plans were going to have to change from what I originally agreed upon. Jared is a guy who is typically quite flexible and accommodating, unless there is food or money involved. I began presenting the emergency-induced change of plans, but before I could get the "We're not going to be able to…" phrase out of my mouth, he erupted with, "We *have* to go to the bank today, Mom! I *have* to get my check cashed!" Messing around with money or food turns Jared into an inflexible contention machine. I weaseled my way through all the *reasons* for the altered plan, and after several attempts ending with my infamous stern face, he finally acquiesced. (By golly, I am still the boss!)

I felt hopeful about a positive ending until I got to the air pump. There she blows – *right next to the highway* – as in literally inches away! Putting air in the tire would require that I get out of our vehicle and squat by the tire in full view of every passing car on the road. I couldn't make Jared do it. Jared had no experience putting air in a car tire, and I wasn't about to talk him calmly through it. I had just spent the entire morning in calm-patient mode trying to help him construct a very detailed Christmas gingerbread house without losing control or consciousness. I would just have to bite the bullet, get out of the car, and in PJs and slippers in 19 degree temperature, do the air pumping myself.

Did I mention I hadn't worked an air pump in years? My husband always did the air-pumping. Who knew that you had to actually *pay* for air! News to me.

Before I got out of the car, though, another thought hit me – I would still be in pajamas upon reaching Big O. Men run Big O. Good grief! I absolutely could not walk into the Big O Tire store in flannel pajamas and slippers! That would be bordering on indecent exposure, at least according to the male gender in a *tire store* who would be witnessing a sixty-plus-year-old woman in flannel PJs walk into their establishment around noon! Being enormously embarrassed doesn't cover it. I think this is what they term as being in a giant pickle.

Rethinking my original plan, and after silently saying my twenty-third prayer before reaching the air pump, I figured that if the good Lord was willing, maybe the air that I put in the tire might hold long enough for me to drive back to our house where I could throw on some clothes before going into the man's world at Big O. That was the new plan.

When I pulled into our garage with a rather disgruntled, hungry, no-check-cashing-in-the-near-future Jared, I instructed him to stay put in the car. I jumped out and quickly checked the tire. It was still up and holding air. Hallelujah!

Just as I headed for the door to the house, my cell phone rang. I ran back to the car, grabbed it out of my purse and answered it. It was Lee. He had gotten my flat tire message. He was fully aware of my flat tire expertise, which is zero. He started giving me the twenty-question conversation. At that moment, I was in huge frustration mode. My heart was racing. I tried to be as polite as possible in letting him know that I had to get off the phone so I could run into the house and change my pajamas before the tire went flat again.

I just made it to the back door when my cell rang a second time. It was my 90 year old dad. Before I could speak, he asked if I wouldn't mind traveling down to his little city to get him some milk and orange juice. He was out. My dad hardly ever asks me for favors, so while rushing in the house toward my closet I'm beginning to experience the "you're a big fat heel" sensation knowing full well I wouldn't be able to help him. During my dad's favor-asking, I tore off my PJs with one hand while trying to hold the phone in the other. He commented, "You sound out of breath, honey."

Understatement. I filled him in on the situation and he backed off the milk and orange juice idea. He said it could wait.

I finished dressing in record time and made it back to the garage. I checked the tire. It was still up. Praise the Lord! Me (now in street clothes), the dog, and Jared all headed out once again.

My brain was still racing, trying to anticipate each course of action I would need to deal with in order to make it to Big O before the tire lost too much air. It occurred to me that I would not be able to get Jared's Burger King chicken sandwich until much later, and it was *lunchtime!* I had already faced the first Jared crisis, the not-going-to-the-bank crisis, now there was an even bigger crisis looming – and this one involved food!

To make matters worse, I realized I was in for more trouble as we neared the gym. He was going to have to walk to work *from the side of the curb*. This was another alteration of the original plan – a third modification. Things were going to get ugly. (Like I said, no cake walk.)

After I spilled the beans on my plans, with a look of utter astonishment on his face, he sputtered, "What?"

Logic has never been one of Jared's strong points. With all the explaining in the world, it still didn't alter the fact that I had just made three revisions to our original plan, and that had the same effect on his mental stability at the moment as murdering an innocent animal. I could see that he was *trying* to accept all the changes, but it was taking its toll. The "walking to work" was the kicker. You would have thought I had asked him to walk to Alaska. Walking from the curbside to the actual gym is approximately 100 feet, tops.

I pulled over to the side of the road to let Jared out. Halfheartedly, he made the effort to dislodge himself from the seat belt. Gradually, he bent down to retrieve his fanny pack from the car floor. As he spent at least a full minute down there groping for it, I swear that I could hear the air hissing out of the tire with each passing second. Ever so slowly, he opened the car door. At last, both feet were planted on asphalt, but he stopped short, turned around and leisurely reached for his huge 44 ounce drink in the console cup holder. I thought I was going to throw a rod! There are times that I honestly believe an earthworm moves faster than my son.

The tire stayed up, Jared finally got out of the car, and I made it to Big O dressed in street clothes. Although I still felt a little weird since the red faded bandana was still on my head and I had not one ounce of make-up on my face. Here is some crucial information: I am not a natural beauty. It takes a massive amount of beauty aids coupled with years of mastered techniques to get me to a five rating (out of ten). The Big O attendant's face spoke volumes as to my appearance. But I am now old and wise – I did not care what that young whippersnapper thought. The tire would soon be fixed. Life was good.

If the truth be known, I was actually on my second day without an ounce make-up. The day before had totally been eaten up wrapping at least a gazillion Christmas presents as well as attempting to put up Christmas lights in Jared's downstairs apartment – tangled lights, non-sticking sticky hooks, and a wrenched neck – but that's another story.

I made it to Burger King, bought Jared's chicken sandwich, also purchased a chicken salad for myself, dropped his lunch off, made it home, walked through our door totally exhausted and collapsed into a kitchen chair! After a few long, deep breaths, I mustered enough oomph to get off the chair and turn on the kitchen lights. *Flick, flick ...flick, flick.* The lights did not work. The entire set of kitchen canister lights would not turn on. But that's another story – back to the salad.

Trying to see in semi-darkness, I dumped the salad into the bowl to add dressing and toss. I looked at my salad. Something was wrong. Where's the chicken? I was certain I had ordered the *chicken* salad. Doggone it! I am not vegan. I happen to be an enthusiastic and devoted meat-eater. Oh well, I put the dressing on my now total veggie salad and ate every drop. I was famished from the morning's ordeal. It wasn't until I had finished eating and was cleaning up that I noticed the empty Burger King sack did not feel empty. There was still something in the bottom of the sack. I looked inside and pulled out a bag with the words "chicken pieces" on the label.

I have learned a couple of things after experiencing this Bad Day, other than proof that Satan is running amok. First of all, I believe I am finally learning how to evaluate and consequently handle things that are basically out of my control, without going ballistic. But I have also learned I have a long way to go. This learning thing seems to be an on-going and eternal process. Shoot!

And secondly, I think I know why Jared chose to come to our household in the very beginning – he could see our character flaws and figured we would need a lot of help in many crucial areas. He knew that by helping him, we would gain greater patience, keener focus, patience, fortitude, patience and empathy – and let's not forget patience. He was right.

"...continue in patience until ye are perfected." DC 67:13

Grandma: "If he doesn't do what I told him to do, he is going to be mud in my eye!"

30

"Find the Joy"

"We cannot direct the wind ...but we can adjust the sails."
~ Author Unknown

When would you feel *joy*? Would you feel it after breaking a leg while skiing? Would you experience it after having a heart attack? Maybe feeling totally broke and destitute might do the trick. No? What about after you learn the company you work for eliminated your job?

You mean not one of these situations brings to mind the word *joy*? Well then, let me help. It might seem a little difficult at first, but I guarantee that you will *eventionally* (as Jared would put it) *"find the joy."*

ॐ

There was this guy. He happened to be a remarkably cool man. What made him so cool comprised two dichotic characteristics. First of all, he was intellectually gifted. Advanced placement chemistry and physics were his teaching specialties at the high school level. However, he had an enormous sense of humor. Now normally, the word "humor" doesn't fit anywhere near the vicinity of words like "physics" or "chemistry," but he was a walking contradiction of terms. Not only did this brilliant man enjoy a good laugh, he loved making other people laugh. He was bit of a tease, full of energy, was witty, kind, and handsome. Quite an awesome package was Jared's Uncle Fred. Lots of pluses.

But what completed the "Fred package" was that he genuinely liked people, and people liked him. He had this remarkable draw, like a little human magnet. Folks sort of oozed out of the woodwork wanting his attention or expertise. The neat thing about him was that he was ever willing and even eager to help whomever, whenever. That's just how he was.

His students were a little miffed that he didn't stay in teaching – they loved him. But his career kept escalating. One promotion put him into the school counselor's position, another advanced him to vice-principal, and he ended up as the school district's assistant superintendant.

Unfortunately, the tide changed. It tends to do that when least expected. It happened to be his LDS bishop who first recognized the signs of Alzheimer's disease. The medical tests confirmed it. At that time, Fred was only 64. On average, that's very early for the onset of this cruel disease. It was a terrible blow to his three grown boys, his grandchildren, and especially to my sister, Mike, his wife.

I share the following story because of its significance. An earnest prayer was said; an answer was received. As a result of that answer, Mike became a rock through what normally would be a depressing, disheartening and discouraging Alzheimer's caregiving experience. Consequently, her experience ended up having a profound effect on my own life. I believe it will have an impactful influence on others who are encountering similar challenges – maybe even you. This is my purpose for sharing this incredible story.

Mike's Story

"After having taken care of Fred for years and watching each little piece of him disappear from this life, things got more and more difficult. Every single day and night was consumed with his care. The beginning of each new day was like stepping into dark, unknown territory – not being able to see where I was going. I often

prayed and talked to Heavenly Father telling Him of my worries, fears and needs. The wonderful thing was that my prayers were always answered. Moving forward was only possible due to those blessed answers. I realized I had to take things one step at a time, even if it was into the unknown.

"One day as I was driving.....in the quiet.....with Fred by my side (as always), I began to feel very down and sad about my situation. The doctor had recently told me that people with this condition can live for up to 20 years in this state. Oh my! There goes my life, I thought! It was terribly unnerving to be at my age and looking at 20 years ahead. Questions like "Would I die first, leaving him to be cared for by others?" or "What would happen to our finances, our home if I had to put him in a care center?" Literature about those things told me that at the point of having to have him cared for I'd need to begin selling things. Selling things? There goes my life.......again! I wondered if I would eventually even lose my home. These thoughts brought great fear to me.

"As I drove in the car with him that day, I prayed to Heavenly Father about my fears and sadness. I was having a huge sad self day. I knew, however, that He'd understand, that He might give me a little pat on the back to let me know somehow that my sadness was understood and that I would feel his great compassion for me and my situation. Instead, as I exited the freeway, (I remember the exact spot where I got this impression) this powerful response came...."This is your life now ...find the joy."

"That was it!

"Although it sounds rather small – or actually, no help at all – this impression and those exact words had a profound impact on me and my situation. I pondered what had just happened to me and the words I had been given. I now had a feeling of taking back power and control. Just moments before I had felt like everything was being taken from me, that I couldn't hang on to anything, not even for myself. This new guidance (or impression) helped me understand that I had control of my life and my circumstances more than I had thought.

*"I continued to ponder.....for days, weeks....about this idea. I learned that the things that happen in this life that we have no control over can cause us to fear, and fear serves no other purpose than to make us feel helpless and hopeless. Eventually impressions came to me to understand that this life was MINE. I needed to **embrace** my situation. I needed to find a way to find the joy in it and continue to move forward. This was an extremely freeing feeling. I learned that there **is** joy to be had.*

As I moved forward with those thoughts and convictions, I found myself feeling joy in my heart at the little fun things of every day. Certainly the things I was experiencing were sometimes actually funny and laughable. I felt hope rising and taking the place of the fear of the unknown. I learned to take each day by itself and not worry about tomorrow. I found moments to be very happy with my children and grandchildren nearby; I had much to be grateful for. As those feelings grew in me, I found more and more ways to move forward in my situation. Learning to ask questions.....lots of questions, of professional people who could advise me on how to care for my husband as he became more and more unable to care for himself."

That is Mike's story. Now, here's a little pop-quiz to see if you're getting the idea. I would ask that you to play a little "let's pretend." See if you can put yourself in the following situation:

Your spouse has Alzheimer's. Caring for him/her is unbelievably demanding and extremely taxing. Doing the simplest things, like fixing a sandwich or emptying the garbage, has now become complicated just trying to keep track of your spouse while doing it. Attempting to accomplish your morning ritual of getting ready for the day is next to impossible. You find it has to be done in increments so you can care for your spouse and give the pressing attention he/she needs between combing your hair, brushing your teeth, and taking your shower. And then it's your spouse's turn for the morning ritual!

You've finished both morning routines, fixed and ate breakfast, did the dishes, and as you glance out the kitchen window you notice a brown spot in the back corner of the lawn. It needs a good dose of water. The problem is that you are already losing steam: you're tired from performing the morning rituals, a bit frustrated after searching for the "hidden" cell phone that your spouse tucked under the couch cushion, a little out of breath after cleaning up the tipped upside down bowl of oatmeal which ended up being "finger-painted" onto the countertop, and the grandfather clock hasn't bonged the 10:00 am hour yet. But that brown spot needs attention. You take a deep breath and head outside with your spouse following close behind (as he/she tends to do these days).

You go to the opposite end of the yard where the hose caddy sits with two lengths of hose coiled on it. You attach the portable rainbird on the end and start walking out to the other side of the yard, unraveling the long hose as you go. Your spouse is still following your every step.

Another predicament is about to crop up. The neighbor's truck sits a few feet from where you need to place the rainbird. It's all shiny – looks like it has just been washed and waxed. In order to end up not watering his newly washed and waxed vehicle you'll need to adjust the rainbird with the water *on*. But the water spigot is around the corner of the house, out of sight. Someone needs to man the spigot while you give the "on" and "off" command. Your spouse is standing right by your side, smiling and happy to be part of what you are doing. Recent experience has shown that sometimes he/she can understand certain simple commands. You're hoping this is the case today.

You instruct your spouse to go around the corner of the house and turn on the water spigot. Your spouse seems to understand these instructions and off he/she goes, disappearing around the corner of the house. Now your focus is on the rainbird, waiting for the water to burst forth so you can adjust the setting without drenching your neighbor's shiny truck. Still waiting... anticipating the water bursting forth. You need to be ready when it comes.

Suddenly you sense a presence behind you. You turn

around and your spouse is smiling, holding the detached end of the first length of hose in his/her hand waiting for further instructions. Your spouse is still happy, still smiling. A little sighing noise escapes your lips. You gently take the hose and tread back to where it was separated. You reattach it.

"Let's give this another try," you say with a smile. (You have learned that smiling is absolutely magical to your spouse's well being. So many things these days confuse him/her that a smile not only calms and comforts your spouse, but does wonders for you, too.) You explain once again that you want the water "turned on" and then make a looping motion with your hand indicating the need to go around the corner of the house where the spigot is located. Your spouse says "okay" and heads in the proper direction. Once again, you turn around, squat down and wait. Your attention is on the rainbird. You watch for the water. Any second now...

A shadow falls on you. Looking up, you see your spouse standing above you holding the other end of the hose again. You sigh a little deeper, but smile. You're getting used to being patient. You have learned to be flexible and tolerant. Evidently, you need to explain things more clearly. So you take the hose back again, your spouse still following you as you reattach it. This time you position your spouse by the spigot. You point directly at it, make a turning motion with your hand, and reiterate that you want the water turned "on" when you give the word. Your spouse confirms with a nod and you quickly head back to ready yourself at the rainbird in case he/she turns it on too soon. Watching. Waiting ...waiting. Nothing is happening. You turn around. There is your spouse standing above you holding the unattached hose from the spigot end.

Here's the $24,000 question: At this point, how would you feel? What would you do?

Want to know what Mike's reaction was? She paused for just a second or two, and then started to laugh. At her reaction, Fred started to laugh. She laughed harder. He laughed harder. They both were in the corner of the yard laughing so hard they had to hang on to the fence post to stay upright.

I wonder if you see the same thing I do when looking at an ostrich? An ostrich is proof positive that the Lord has a sense of humor. I think the ostrich is our biggest tip as to the importance of seeing the humor in things. After all, we were actually meant to be happy – we were meant to smile. *"...men are, that they might have joy." (2 Nephi 2:25)*

Back to the question, "When would you feel joy?" The secret is in the *finding*. The joy is there. You need to separate it from all of life's minutia, clutter, chaos and catastrophes.

In the book *The Road Less Traveled* by M. Scott Peck, he says: "Life is difficult. This is a great truth. Perhaps the greatest of all the truths. Because once we understand it, then we can transcend it." (The "transcend it" part of that sentence is vital, so take note.) He goes on, "Most do not fully see this truth that life is difficult. Instead they moan more or less incessantly, noisily, or subtly, about the enormity of their problems, their burdens, and their difficulties as if life were generally easy, as if life *should* be easy."

Mike now knows this. She learned to *"find the joy."*

Late one evening, Mike was comfortably lying in bed watching one of her favorite British comedies on TV. Fred was quietly snoozing next to her. The quiet, the calm, and the chuckles were the therapy needed after another long day caring for her sweet husband. She started to feel a little sleepy but was reluctant to let go of the peace and joy of the moment. As usually happens with most of us at that late hour, Morpheus' enticements won out. She just couldn't stay awake any longer. Sighing, she reached for the long black remote to shut down the TV and call it a night.

It wasn't there. She checked all the usual places. No long black remote. Gently pulling back the sheets to see if it was hiding within the bed confines brought no success. She even looked inside of Fred's favorite hiding place: his boots. No luck. It was nowhere to be found. But dealing with Alzheimer's 24/7 had taught her not to stress over the small stuff. The long black remote would turn up eventually. So she manually pushed the power button on the TV and settled in for the evening.

The next morning she began the getting-Fred-into-the-shower routine; first the top comes off, then the pajama bottoms, then the Depends (adult diaper). That's when she experienced her major heart attack. She couldn't breathe – which lasted only a few seconds. It lasted just long enough for the shock to subside so she could see what was actually cradled inside of the front portion of Fred's Depends: the long black remote.

The laughter came after the shock wore off. That's the way of things – at least, these things. But the laughter comes. That's what she learned.

"...I beseech of thee that thou wilt hear my words and learn of me; for I do know that whosoever shall put their trust in God shall be supported in their trials, and their troubles, and their afflictions...."
~ Alma 36:3

We were having trouble trying to find a parking place in a very large multilevel underground parking garage.

Jared commented,
"Just don't park in the middle thirties!"

(He meant "lower forty." If you are a farmer, you know that "lower forty" refers to acreage and means way, way, way out there!)

31

Silver Trumps Gold

"Let me win. But if I cannot win, let me be brave in the attempt."
~ Special Olympian Oath

If Eunice Kennedy Shriver were alive today, I would kiss her full on the lips! What a compassionate, benevolent woman! She probably had no idea that what she started in her backyard back in 1962 would have had such a huge impact – the inception of Special Olympics. She is a saint in my eyes.

If you have never taken the opportunity to watch Special Olympians during the heat of competition, you've missed the big boat. It is an unforgettable experience. And after watching them for so many years, I found out something that was quite remarkable. There is no difference between the athletic spirit of a Special Olympian, and the athletic spirit of your average Olympic athlete. Wait – there is that one thing – the one special thing that sets them apart: those faces! They're priceless! Those inimitable Special Olympians just can't hide their over-the-top enthusiasm – that unabashed thrill of competing in the big Special O. I love that they let it all hang out – even *before* the competition begins! It is totally infectious. You simply cannot watch a Special Olympian compete without inadvertently developing a huge smiling heart. It just happens. What a joyous experience!

Another thing that makes them stand out is the way they view being an athlete. It isn't taken for granted. To be called "athlete" outright is a thrill in and of itself. To them, it is such an honor.

It had been over 25 years since Jared had participated in Special Olympics Track and Field. He had been content participating in a variety of regular community youth sports events through the years, but up to this point in time, his sole Special Olympic involvement had been in bowling. If truth be known, it was the socialization in the pit (the bench area where bowlers sit and chew the fat waiting for their turn) that lit his fire. Rolling the ball down the alley was fairly fun, but it was the magical mix of team camaraderie, back slapping, knuckle bumps, fries and that extra large Diet Coke that was the clincher. This year, however, he decided to branch out and add track and field to his Special Olympic repertoire. That troubled me.

Signing up for track and field meant running races. In his youth, Jared's bout with Legg Perthes disease left him with one leg shorter than the other. That's not a plus for running efficacy. His knees weren't so great either. The orthopedic surgeon made it clear that any jarring would injure his knees that were already close to rubbing bone on bone. Running equaled jarring. But Jared told me he could participate in the walking events. The walking races wouldn't jar his already jinxed joints.

But there was an additional fly in the worry ointment. There would always be that ever present temptation for him to cut loose and let 'er rip. You see, Jared was fully capable of running full bore; he just wasn't *supposed* to. I was concerned that if his coach ever happened to be out of supervision range, Jared might surrender to the enticement of sprinting around the track with wings on his feet and the wind in his hair. But he made a solemn vow that he would stay in control. I believed him. That cinched the deal. Track and field, here comes Jared.

For the past couple of months, the Golden Spikers' team, of which Jared and Jessie were a part, had been vigorously training for the event. Now they were ready. Today was their big day.

It was a beautiful – though way too early for my taste – clear spring morning when Jared, Jessie, Betty (Jessie's mother) and

I headed to the Special Olympics Track and Field event. Half of the drive involved a trip through the canyon. This time of year is always absolutely breathtaking in those majestic edifices. The mountainous foliage was well on its way turning from dull winter gray to a vast variant of gorgeously brilliant greens that were absolutely stunning. Their fresh and colorful springtime attire was in stark contrast to the lustrous white snow that still tenaciously clung to their lofty peeks. That exhilarating morning drive alone was worth rolling out of bed before the crack of dawn.

From the university parking lot, our little foursome hobbled along as we headed to the track and field arena lugging folding chairs, water bottles, snack cooler, blankets, daypacks, coats, an assortment of hats, and an umbrella (just in case). We finally made it to our team's little corner of the world, gratefully plunking all our paraphernalia down on a nice grassy spot close to the edge of the track and settled in.

A hush fell over the spectators as the coaches' recited their traditional and heartfelt pledge. Next came the athlete's oath, recited in mass by the athletes themselves. What a stirring moment! But the pinnacle of the opening was the Torch Run. What a majestic, awesome sight! It stimulates every molecule and sensation in the human heart. Totally awesome!

Since Jared's first event wasn't scheduled until just before lunch, we sat back in our comfy portable chairs with sunscreen slathered over blindingly white sun-starved skin, drinks at the ready, content on watching the upcoming action.

It wasn't one of your warmer spring mornings. Even though it was practically a cloudless day, there was a definite nip in the air. It made us appreciate the sun's warm rays as well as the blankets we remembered to bring. As we all relaxed by the side of the track, my mind traveled back to the benevolence of Eunice and why she had that backyard party in the first place. Because of her sister Rose's intellectual disability, Eunice saw how people like her sister were excluded, ignored, and often neglected. They hardly had an opportunity to win at anything. This gave her an idea, she set a goal, and as Michael Jackson so poignantly sang, *healed the world* —

made it a better place. Bless her.

Today, though, (and this might shock you as much as it did me) the main goal of Special Olympics isn't winning – it said so right on their web page. "Winning and losing are beside the point" is how they put it. The Special Olympics' goal is "to build confidence, skill and fitness in their athletes through training and competition." Now that is certainly admirable. But it is very clear they did not know Jared and Jessie. Evidently, Jared and Jessie didn't get the memo. Those two are totally focused on *winning the gold!* To them, winning a fourth, fifth, or sixth place ribbon just doesn't cut it. Why *is* that? I'm thinkin' it's probably a byproduct of the inadvertent brainwashing by the National Olympics' resounding phrase "Go for the gold!" For Jared and Jessie, taking first place (i.e standing proudly on block #1 as that gold medal is placed around their neck) is the pinnacle in their competitive world.

Yet today would be different. Today would change things for Jared. This day, silver would come out on top.

This track and field thing was marvelous! It was nothing like the bowling thing. All those years watching Jared participate in bowling conditioned me to the routine of that type of competition. There were always cheers for a strike or a spare, but in the interim there was just standard socialization and chitchat amongst the athletes. But with this track and field thing, there was *"...and they're off!"* followed by jumping and shouting and cheering and whistling and air pumping. The atmosphere was absolutely electric! And with so much more physical exertion involved, watching the athletes in this type of event threw me into a totally different mindset.

Among some of the Special Olympians that passed by us in the races was a girl with rigid legs who could only walk on the balls of her feet, an older gentleman with a rather crooked spine and a distinct limp, a middle-aged man with a contorted and awkward gait, a relatively corpulent boy who ran with one hand hanging onto his waistband so his pants wouldn't fall down, and a tall skinny man with an exuberant smile who was more interested in Queen-Elizabeth-crowd-waving than crossing the finish line, and there were so many others. With the exception of the waving guy, these Special Olympians showed such incredible courage and determination by disregarding their physical flaws by putting their whole hearts and souls into the competition. These folks were awesome!

Jared won his first race, the 100 meter walk, by a healthy lead. It was then that the pangs of guilt hit me. My son was competing against these folks – my son, who had no *visible* physical disability with which to contend, who happened to look in top physical condition due to years of regular workouts at the gym, and who had been blessed with the joy of participating in community team sports several years running. Remember that he even received a standing ovation during a basketball game ("The Long Shot" chapter). On a regular basis he had experienced the moral support, high fives, and back patting from his community teammates. But these Special Olympic athletes probably hadn't had the luxury or the opportunity to taste the gratification or respect that Jared had been exposed to most of his life. Thank heaven above they had Special Olympics in which to shine. *(An especially big hug for Ms. Shriver.)*

When one of the guest firemen placed the gold medal around Jared's neck, I had mixed emotions. He looked so happy to have won, but did he snatch happiness away from someone who needed it more? I felt conflicted – a traitor to these special Olympians, and yet a traitor to my son as well. I was extremely uncomfortable with it all.

The time came to break for lunch. All the athletes scurried over to the chow table where they were treated to a complimentary lunch. We onlookers came equipped with our own homemade lunches. I drooled a little when Jared and Jess came back with their delightfully packed plates, colorful energy drinks and broad smiles. Their Special Olympic cuisine looked a heck of a lot more appealing than my own brown-bag of victuals.

As I took a bite out of my first Wheat Thin, I could barely hear the announcer when she introduced a young man who seemed to be the object of a half-time event. The crowd quieted slightly, and I was able to hear the announcer say, "He will take three small balls, then one large ball and put them in the bucket." *What*? I couldn't see what was going on because of all the wandering bodies blocking my view. But... did I hear correctly?

There was a short pause, and then the announcer roared excitedly, "Therrrrre goes the first. A direct hit!" The crowd cheered. *What in the world was so great about someone putting a ball in a bucket?*

A second short pause was followed by another declaration that ball number two had made it into the bucket. More crowd clapping and cheering.

It was then that the meandering crowd parted slightly and I spotted the announcer standing next to a very thin young man who was in a wheelchair. This guy had contorted arms and legs that looked more like plucked chicken wings than normal limbs. As he attempted to pick up ball number three, the grueling strain on his face was apparent – he was using every ounce of concentration he could muster in trying to make his rigid arms and hands unfold enough to pick up the third small ball, move it ever so slightly forward, and command his unyielding crooked hands to release it into the bucket. Another roaring cheer from the crowd.

I felt so totally embarrassed by my initial insensitive attitude toward the ball in the bucket event. I am such a doof at times!

After each ball landed successfully in the bucket, and after the subsequent clapping and cheering permeated the air, this young man's entire body literally vibrated with uncontained exhilaration. His vibrating was accompanied by a wide massively humongous smile. I doubt there was anywhere else on this planet he would have felt as important or as proud as here at this magical event with such a conglomeration of caring people appreciating his efforts with the auditory display of approval and praise. *(Another big hug for Eunice!)*

...Back to Jared and his 200 meter walk race, which was the last event of the day. He and the other five Special Olympians in his heat were positioning themselves at the starting line. I was becoming more uncomfortable by the minute. It occurred to me that Jared would probably zoom past all the other competitors, just as he had done in his last race. He didn't have a limp, or stiff legs, a club foot, or an awkward gait. He looked so capable. He didn't fit the mold for this special event. It was like he was stealing the thunder from the other athletes. I promised myself that next year I would try to persuade him into forgoing the walking races and trying the shot-put or softball throw instead. But for now, the race was on.

Boom! They were off. Standing on the sideline I watched for Jared to round the bend. There he came and was now heading straight toward me. Sure enough, he had the lead, but one of his own teammates, who we'll call Leslie, was close behind. When he noticed how close she was, he pushed for a little more speed. Just as they passed me, something strange happened. Jared started slowing down! *What was he doing?* He didn't look tired, he wasn't hurt, he didn't seem confused, yet he was definitely putting on the breaks. It was too early for him to be so confident – he was still several yards away from the finish line. I was thoroughly confused.

Due to his unexpected slowdown Leslie realized she was now gaining ground. Her expression was one of surprise. Next came an intense focus which paved the way to dogged determination. Jared and Leslie were now neck and neck, closing fast on the finish line. He wasn't even trying to pick up his pace! Then I saw the look on his face. It suddenly occurred to me what was happening. I knew Jared. I got it.

From my standpoint, it looked like a photo finish. I couldn't be sure if one had crossed the finish line ahead of the other. Only the timers knew for sure, and as per instructed by the Special Olympic directive, their lips were zipped. The official results would be announced only at the winners circle (or rather, at the "mound of numbered blocks").

Jared and Leslie, still a little breathless from their race, ambled over to the awards area. I followed close behind.

The spokesman began awarding their race: sixth place to begin with, then fifth. After third place was announced, I could see that Leslie was holding her breath with her knuckles pressed to her lips. She knew that if Jared's name was called before hers, it would mean that she had won the gold.

And there it was: Jared's name was announced as second place winner.   Leslie let out a scream that could be heard in Lithuania. Jared climbed up on block #2. As the silver medal was placed over Jared's head, Leslie was proclaimed the gold medalist. She screamed again …and again. She kept screaming and bobbing up and down, literally bouncing onto the coveted first place award block. (Evidently, she hadn't received the memo about winning not being top priority either.)

Jared had the sweetest smile on his face. As the gold medal was placed over Leslie's head, Jared reached up and patted her shoulder.   She put her arm over his shoulder and hugged him through giggles and more bobbing.

At home, later that evening, I went into Jared's room. His two medals were on his dresser. I picked them up and sat next to him on his bed. I asked him how he felt when the gold medal was placed around his neck. He said, "I felt really good, Mom. I felt really happy." Then I asked him how he felt when the gold medal was placed around Leslie's neck after his second race. With a sly little smile, he said, "I felt even better." I gave him a bear hug.

I have since framed those two medals, side by side, as a constant reminder to him of what he did that day: what was *really* important. I always want him to remember the feelings he had that trumped "going for the gold."

That day, I learned a lot about Special Olympians. That day, I learned that the late Eunice Kennedy Shriver was my new hero. And that day, I learned a little more about my own son's benevolence.

"My fruit is better than gold, yea, than fine gold; and my revenue than choice silver." ~ Proverbs 8:19

Grandma's Crooked Cliché

"Sticks and stones may break my bones,
but birds will never hurt me!"

32

A Proliferation of Problematical Stuff

If I could wish for my life to be perfect, it would be tempting, but I would have to decline, for life would no longer teach me anything.
~ *Allyson Jones*

It was a mild summer morning in 1993, rather balmy as summer mornings go, though typically black as pitch at the 4:00 A.M. time slot. The sun wouldn't be up for another three to four hours. Our furry family member, Max, was priming himself for our routine predawn walk by relentlessly bouncing up and down at my feet. The rest of the household happened to be deep in slumberland.

Though Max and I thoroughly enjoyed each other's company on these customary walks, two things challenged my resolve every single morning: First, the "rising inhumanly early" part (which was always tough and grew more difficult with each passing year); and secondly, walking around in the dark for over an hour was not necessarily appealing either, especially during those rainy/snowy/windy/generally rotten weather days. But I was determined. I was committed. Our loyal little Max deserved an aerobic outing. So did I.

Incidentally, those walks actually used to be runs. I loved to run. Max *really* loved to run. But we had been viscously attacked by Father Time. He assaulted us with bad knees, bad backs, bad hips and bad paws. Plus, during our running years, the unforgiving asphalt beneath our pounding little paws hadn't done us any favors. Darn that asphalt, and double darn that old Father Time guy! Ultimately, we were forced to resign ourselves to the slower, less injurious pace.

That particular morning, a mere half block after walking out our front door, something strange hit me. It wasn't a badly aimed newspaper, a runaway milk truck, or a low hanging tree branch – nothing that tangible. I felt dizzy. I felt nauseous. With each step, it got worse. Spinning in one's head is never a good sign. Could it be the flu? Doing a quick 180° I headed for home dragging my baffled little leashed pooch behind me. He hadn't even had time to inaugurate his first tree.

If you would have told me that life as I knew it would change forever within those next few minutes, I wouldn't have believed you. But it did. I barely made it into the house and up the stairs to the bathroom, wrapping my arms around the toilet bowl before my equilibrium totally vanished. Gone! One minute I had been reasonably normal, and the next minute my world was in a tailspin – quite literally, and quite permanently.

Sitting on the floor holding on to that toilet bowl was my only means of stability. I couldn't tell up from down. The spinning in my head was so insidious that I couldn't think. My eyes pinched tightly shut as I kept a death grip on the bowl. When my arms started going numb, I tried loosening my grip. Total disorientation took over. I flailed and thrashed about until I once again found the toilet bowl and resumed a firm hold. It was one of the most horrific things I had ever experienced.

It wasn't the flu. Later, a specialist would diagnose the culprit as a microscopic bully of a bug (a virus) that fortuitously found its way into my inner ear and attacked my once normal balance nerve. I had no idea this condition ever existed. Now I was experiencing it firsthand.

As time went on, a little of my equilibrium returned, but the virus had permanently destroyed over 95% of the balance nerve in my right ear. I tried all sorts of remedies; medication, acupuncture, herbs, physical therapy, change in diet, eventually even brain surgery, but nothing worked. I was destined to be forever dizzy. I ended up being part of an ugly statistic.

You might have noticed that I didn't list prayer as one of the aforementioned remedies. You have now reached a point in the book where you know that praying would have been first on my list. It was. I continued to do it, fervently, but evidently this was an experience I needed to have. That enlightenment was certainly not appealing. I would rather this dizzy ailment be gone. But there were special lessons I needed to learn, and this would be the vehicle. I wouldn't know exactly what I was to learn until I had experienced more, and until those experiences fermented a bit. But the lessons came.

I had always thought of myself as a fairly tough lady. I liked being physically fit and emotionally strong. Toughness seemed to be an admirable quality. I had been an athlete a good part of my life. Because of this, pain was not foreign to me. It was something I could handle. Dealing with pain was do-able, even meritorious. You could conquer pain and come out on top, or at least be praised for the effort. This was not pain. This was annoyingly different – maddeningly, exasperatingly different. With this dizzying detriment I didn't feel tough or fit or strong. I felt helpless. I felt vulnerable. It turned me into a big pusillanimous wimpy marshmallow.

To add to my pickle, it wasn't consistent. Some days it became a lot worse. Barometric pressure fluctuations aggravated it. You probably think I'm off my rocker. Not so. I have since learned this proven fact: changes in barometric pressure wreak havoc with those of us who have certain issues, like my husband for instance. Though he isn't dizzy prone, he is plagued with tinnitus (ringing in his ears). When pressure changes occur, he gets buzzing so badly that he can hardly hear.

It isn't all doom and gloom, however. There is actually an upside to both our maddening maladies. We can predict weather changes! I am dead serious. Together we are more accurate with our predictions than those classy well paid weather forecasters you see on TV, and neither of us had to fork out a single penny for climatology classes or pricey weather gadgets. It works like this: when I suddenly start walking into walls and he starts doing his *Eh?, Huh?,* and *What?* routine, these things are definitive proof weather changes are forthcoming. We are totally accurate 100% of the time! Weather forecasting. Who would have thought?

Those atmospheric variants even affect most children, and the poor little kids don't even know it! Think I'm pulling your leg? Go check with the nearest elementary school teacher, or talk with any day cashier at a grocery store, or any mother who has put two-and-two together. They are unenthusiastic witnesses to children in their general vicinity going nuts prior to a brewing storm. The proof is in the proliferation of spiked-up yelling, crying, temper-tantruming, and general run-amoking by kids that occur on those change-in-the-weather days. I found that incredibly bizarre, but absolutely true.

Years later, the lessons I was to learn from this dizzy disadvantage finally came. It happened during a talk given by Levi. Levi is a handsome, sweet young man who is a member of the Special Needs Mutual. When he is assigned to speak at one of SNM's itinerant Sacrament Meeting presentations, he always gives an eye-opener talk, one that has everyone's rapt attention.

He begins by informing the congregation that he was born nearly four months early and weighed less than two pounds. Because of his too early earthly appearance, he has experienced a myriad of health problems. As he speaks (and plays a beautiful piano piece) it is obvious he has overcome these obstacles and has done so with dignity, courage and fortitude.

I thought about his challenges while he spoke and the poem "Invictus" by William Ernest Henley appeared in my head. It became apparent that Levi was the perfect personification of that poem, especially the last stanza: "It matters not how strait the gate, how charged with punishments the scroll, I am the master of my fate; I am the captain of my soul." At that moment it became crystal clear that it isn't the severity, the nature, or even the number of challenges with which we must deal that matter, it is *how we deal with them* that makes all the difference. Not just experiencing, but *dealing* with these various problems are a crucial and a very necessary part of our growth – they're part of our earthly instruction period. I believe it's our indoctrination to humility as well as chutzpah. Another vital lesson learned! But there were more lessons to come.

Let me share another epiphany that came while Levi was speaking. It was this: Levi wasn't the only one who was handicapped, neither was my son. I realized that I, too, had a handicap! This was huge. This realization forced me look at everything and everyone around me so differently. Then, another epiphany followed: I realized that every person, every single person on this planet, has a handicap. Out in the world there are a vast potpourri of handicaps (to one degree or another), and every human being has at least one.

Some handicaps are visible, like Jared's, or the boy's in the wheelchair at the Special Olympics track and field event. Some handicaps are not physically discernible, like mine or my husband's, or those folks who have other internal ailments or mental issues. Some handicaps are not permanent, others may be periodic. But every single person I know of has some sort of obstacle with which they have to deal. This was lightning bolt clear to me!

I used to be someone who did spins, leaps, and handstands on a 3" balance beam four feet off the floor. Now I can't walk a straight line on the ground. I used to be a member of the women's volleyball team in college. Now whenever I look upward without holding onto something, I lose all equilibrium and flip backward. Even when I attempt to run a few steps, everything in my visual panorama bounces with each step. And because this handicap is not visible, nobody is the wiser – nobody can tell that I have it. Here is where the *dealing with it effectively* comes into play. It's not easy. I don't think it was meant to be. It is a covert culprit. I no longer feel strong – I no longer feel tough. There are times I feel like a monolithic milquetoast.

I am a regular prayer-type person. However, the *dealing with* aspect of this dizzy dilemma makes me hit my knees even more often. It is *because* I feel like a monolithic milquetoast.

Heavenly Father will not allow us to suffer through anything He feels we cannot handle. I know that to be true. Though that doesn't mean we have to suck it up and go it alone to face difficult challenges. The Lord has said, "And all things, whatsoever ye shall *ask* in prayer, *believing*, ye shall receive" (Matthew 21:22) italics added. I *believe* that. *Believing* means I have *faith* it is true. And I know that faith happens to be an action word. It means that, yes, I have to do my own part in working through it on a day to day basis. However, He *expects* me to ask for help when things get a little too hairy, too hard. There are days after hitting my knees *(asking)* that those earthly angels miraculously appear to help me. Other times, after prayer, the extra strength that I need ...comes. Sometimes I simply get a good shot of inner peace. But I always get what I need when I need it – *after I ask*.

Do not get the wrong idea here. If a magical, somewhat good-looking genie miraculously popped out of one of my Diet Coke bottles to grant me that one coveted wish, I would not hesitate one millisecond to wish this dastardly disorder be gone. But thus far, after opening hundreds of Diet Coke bottles, there has yet to appear a magical genie popping anywhere near my vicinity – handsome, homely, hallucinatory or otherwise. So I'll live with it, but I don't have to like it.

That said, it did do something to me that I very much needed. It humbled me. It made me a better person. I became much more open-minded, a lot more understanding, more patient and appreciative of others who had their own various issues with which they were dealing regardless of what they were. It turned out to be one of the best things that ever happened to me.

There is a poem Levi recites during his talk that's worth sharing. Its catchy rhythmical lyrics by Digby Wolfe are clever and poignant.

The Kids Who Are Different

Here's to the kids who are different,
The kids who don't always get A's
The kids who have ears twice the size of their peers,
And noses that go on for days...
Here's to the kids who are different,
The kids they call crazy or dumb,
The kids who don't fit, with the guts and the grit,
Who dance to a different drum...
Here's to the kids who are different,
The kids with the mischievous streak,
For when they have grown, as history's shown,
It's their difference that makes them unique.

It occurred to me that we are all different, that we are all unique – *just like everybody else.* Lesson learned!

One more thing... before this malady hit me, I realized something unsettling: complacency had silently eased its way into my world. Somewhere along the way I had lost perspective. I hadn't paid attention to everyday-type things, those routine yet magnificent daily gifts, with which I had been blessed: eye sight, hearing, sense of smell, of taste, of touch - even equilibrium. Just being able to get out of bed in the mornings safe and sound, to walk, to talk, to go to the fridge and pull food out, these were all wonderfully remarkable gifts. I had been taking so much for granted without thinking about these common, everyday, blessed things. I no longer would.

"...thou knowest the greatness of God; and he shall consecrate thine
afflictions for thy gain."
~ 2 Nephi 2:2

Grandma: "*It was almost a disastrophy!*"

(disaster/catastrophe – take your pick)

33

Wrapping It Up ...or, Lesson? What Lesson?

"Don't wish it was easier,
Wish you were better.
Don't wish for less problems,
Wish for more skills.
Don't wish for less challenges,
Wish for more wisdom.   ~ Jim Rohn

One fine summer day I took my two grandchildren to McDonald's for a treat – by that I mean that Mickey D would fix their lunch instead of me ...and give them fries. It was one of their favorite places to go since they could deliriously and legally run amok. Many times I have been tempted run amok with them, but I was always a little afraid of getting stuck in one of those colorful tubes.

After walking through the door, it occurred to me that two little people were missing from my side. They were with me but a second ago. How could they get lost between the car door and the entrance? Since I had a few years of grand-parenting under my belt, I was fully aware of the lagging-grandchildren phenomenon, so I didn't panic. I turned around and headed back out the door. There they were – busily cleaning up McDonald's parking lot.

This was a mystery to me. I was pretty sure that Mickey D had its own cleanup crew. Did my six and eight year old grandkids have an under-the-table contract with the clown's establishment to make a little spending money on the side? What?

I was a little slow on the uptake, but I finally got it. They were simply incorporating the advice I had given them earlier at the park. I had picked up a dirty old squashed paper cup that was under the jungle gym, walked over to the nearest trash receptacle and tossed it in. Then, in my most stately and judicious grandmotherly voice I said, "Remember to always leave people, places and things better than you find them."

I have been giving them that type of advice, as well as other gems of wisdom, all their little lives. It's my job. They expect it. I'm Nana. However, for this particular gem, cleaning up McDonald's parking lot wasn't quite what I had in mind. Though their interpretation was a little skewed, they had the general idea. They had learned the lesson.

But they had learned the lesson because Nana told it to them. Unfortunately, as grown-ups, there is no grandma at our elbow to help us "get" life's lessons. It's up to us to find them. And here's the thing – there are lessons in everything, from having one's molars removed, to playing solitaire, or losing a championship game, or buying a home, or dealing with an obnoxious neighbor, or creating a Keish pie, or telling a fib, or being fired, or losing a beloved pet. Lessons are found in the good, the bad, the ugly, the mundane, the unusual, the happy, the sad – there are lessons to be learned in absolutely everything. A wise man once said, "Tragedy is not what we suffer, but what we miss."

Consider this: if what I say is true, that there are lessons in everything, then why aren't we all as smart or as wise as the Dali Lama, Mother Teresa, C. S. Lewis, or Doctor Stephen Hawking?

It is so simple that you'll wonder why you didn't see it before. We don't usually realize there *are* lessons because *we aren't' looking for them!* That's the key – looking for them. Paying attention. Most lessons do not jump out and announce, "I'm right here! Enjoy the gift!" Sometimes they are veiled, subtle. There are times they are elusive. Sometimes they don't show up right away because they need a little fermenting, but they are always there. The secret is being aware there *are* lessons, and... *looking for them!*

Barbara DeAngelis said, "Only when your consciousness is totally focused on the moment you are in can you receive whatever gift, lesson, or delight that moment has to offer." What Ms. DeAngleis is alluding to is that a concerted effort must be made. If not, those wonderful poignant lessons slip away and may be lost forever. And the effort must not only be a conscious one, it must be a habitual one.

After making the effort of asking *"What did I learn from this?"* or *"What's the lesson?"* enough times, it becomes a habit. Once it becomes a habit, the effort needed diminishes. It becomes a natural thought process. And here is the miracle in this process: once you learn the lessons they become part of you, and you become ...*better.*

This Jared journey has made us better. Not just Lee and John and me, but it has made an indelible impression on everyone who has ever been involved in his upbringing, his learning, or even just been around him. We are all better for having him in our lives. Jared is our teacher, our gift. We will be eternally grateful.

"Know thou, my son, that all these things shall give thee experience,
and shall be for thy good."
(D&C 122: 7)

୬୦ବ

Postscript: While we *"learn the lessons,"* let us not forget to keep a sense of humor about things. A sense of humor keeps it all in perspective. At the publication of this book, Phyllis Diller was 96. Betty White was 90. George Burns lived to be 100, so did Bob Hope, and Hope's widow lived to be 102, probably from laughing at him all those years. That's why they lived so long. These are/were all funny people. They all know/knew how to laugh.

Promise me you won't forget to laugh!

*"...a man's wisdom maketh his face to shine,
and the boldness of his face shall be changed." Ecclesiastes 8:1*

"I'm sore from working out today. There's a lot of that Atlantic acid in my muscles."

(lactic acid)

34

Towels, Ear Rubs and the Jitterbug

"The purposes of the Lord in our personal lives generally are fulfilled through the small and simple things, and not the momentous and spectacular." ~ *M. Russell Ballard*

This chapter should not exist. After chapter 32, I was finished, finito, terminé, el-done-o. I was pleased with what I had and was ready to move on to the next step for the book. But a Higher Source had a different idea.

By now you know that I'm a prayer-type person. In the evenings, the focus of my prayers is on gratitude. My morning prayers are the "get down to daily business" prayers. It was during one of my morning prayers that my mind kept wandering to a few extraneous, unrelated thoughts. I couldn't seem to stay focused. Those thoughts persisted in sneaking their way back into my head, over and over again. I was a little puzzled as to why these particular, seemingly unconnected thoughts kept attacking my attempt to concentrate.

As I've said before, sometimes I'm a little slow on the uptake, but I finally got it. I knew what had to be done, and knew it had to be done ASAP. You must not mess around when the Guy Upstairs is giving you ideas, especially during a direct communiqué. So I'm sitting here at my laptop ready to record the thoughts as they occurred to me. Evidently, there must be a few of you out there who are in need of this chapter.

One of the stray thoughts led me to think about Jared's job at Anytime Fitness. That led me to remember how it came about: looking at the gym's hand towels. Picturing those hand towels led me to think of someone who had not crossed my mind in years: Earl.

Earl was a man who was intellectually disabled. He worked at the university gymnasium during my college days. He was the main towel guy. He gathered, washed, dried, folded, stacked, and distributed those towels for years. That was his main job: towels. And he loved it. Most everyone knew Earl, acknowledged him, and respected him. He wasn't just a towel guy; he was *the* towel guy, and a darned good one. He was so proud of his work. From what I was told, he never took a day off nor was he ever late for work.

I wondered if anyone else would have felt the same way about doing that towel job as Earl did. I doubted it. Most people wouldn't like the tedium of doing nothing but towels day in and day out, especially for Earl's wage. Most people would want a change, or would want a raise, or a promotion, or there would be a dependability issue, or they would quit because they were bored. Not Earl. He loved his job, was good at it, was grateful for it, and was proud doing it. Though his job was not considered prestigious by most, his contribution to the university was important. *Towels*.

Along the same line, I thought of a couple of other folks who also had mental disabilities and also had jobs that they loved. They were married to each other and worked at the same restaurant for thirty years peeling potatoes. That's what they did. They peeled potatoes. They were good at their jobs, grateful they had them, and felt proud to work at the restaurant. Moreover, they were a valuable asset to that establishment. *Potatoes*.

I came to a conclusion: Though we are all vastly different in so many ways, there is always something out there for *everyone*. Even dull, tedious, monotonous type jobs that some might hate, others appreciate those jobs and like doing them. Furthermore, those jobs are every bit as important for the success of a business' operation as a CEO's job. How wonderful is that? And what a blessing it is to both parties – the employer and the employee. It's win-win.

Another stray thought involved a little pooch we had several years ago I mentioned earlier. His name was Max. We found him "on the run" so to speak. Like Cooper, our current furry family affiliate, he had been a homeless mutt, i.e. there was no pedigree involved. (Our family tends to be drawn to mutts.) He was a smallish black dog with the body of a dachshund, the fur of a cockapoo, the face of a schnauzer, and the ears of a water spaniel. There was nothing really special about him, except that he was special to us.

One evening, after our family's traditional Saturday night dinner, my husband and I were sitting in the living room chatting with my parents. At the time, my mother was in the later stages of Alzheimer's disease. Max was not aware of Alzheimer's. Dogs do not know these things. But something took us by surprise. Max came trotting in the living room and jumped on my mother's skinny little lap, looking as if he felt right at home. This was not SOP for him. Nor had she made any gesture for him to jump up there. We were stunned. This act was out of character for Max. He was not a lap dog. He hated laps. He didn't fit on laps. His rather elongated middle made lap sitting awkward. Yet there he was, totally content, draped across my mother's lap, head drooping to one side and his rear-end hanging off the other. The way he was positioned he couldn't have looked more uncomfortable. Cats would be okay precariously hanging like that – dogs, not so much.

Then she started rubbing his ears. *Rubbing his ears!* Max hates his ears rubbed! He wouldn't even let me do that, and I'd like to think I was one of his favorite people. Yet he was lying on her lap in this uncharacteristically contorted position letting her rub his ears.

There was something quite remarkable about the whole thing. While she was performing that simple little act, she began to relax. It was soothing to her. It calmed her. (You *know* about the rubbing of fur thing!) You cannot convince me that Max's inclination to head for my mother and jump up on her small skinny-legged lap was not a big deal. There was something more to it.

Here is the last of my stray thoughts. It involved my mother again, only it included Jared. During her bout with Alzheimer's, Mother had become extremely confused. She had forgotten how to do so many things. For a while she was able to set our family dinner table on Saturday nights when we all got together, until she couldn't distinguish a fork from a knife. We found, though, that she could still fold linens. So I made sure I always had a basket of clean towels for her to fold. It kept her engaged, and I think it made her feel like she was contributing. Sadly, however, even the towel folding became too bewildering for her.

Jared didn't fully understand his grandma's condition. Even more confusing for him was her constantly changing limitations. He couldn't keep up with what she could and could not do.

One Saturday night as we sat around the dinner table, Jared stood up and walked over to Grandma, pulled her chair out, took her by the hand, and led her down the hallway. We were all a little puzzled by this. I had no idea what he was planning. On the way, he looked over his shoulder and said, "We're going to my room to dance."

Once in his room, he put a CD into his stereo system and they started to jitterbug. They jitterbugged until they were both sweaty and winded. She had *not* forgotten how to jitterbug! It was so wonderful to peek into his room and see her laughing, singing, jumping and jiving with Jared. For the next few months, that became their after dinner ritual on Saturday nights.

An added bonus to those little jitterbugging sessions was what it did for my dad. It gave him a little peace, a little reprieve. He had the opportunity to relax and enjoy a good uninterrupted chat with us while Jared and Grandma were busy cutting-a-rug down the hall. That dancing idea was no accident, nor was it just an incidental thought.

There is a thread of commonality among all these things. I wonder if you see it?

You might believe that God was involved, as was

compassion, love, selflessness, inspiration, and those earthly angels. That's what I believe. God gifts us with little miracles every single day. We just need to *see* them.

"...out of small things proceedeth that which is great." DC 64:33

൸൸

One last thought: In this game called life, I've learned that we mustn't squat at home base with a catcher's mitt on each hand. I've learned that if we want good to happen, we must be able to throw something back. And the miracle is this: the more we throw back, the more we get. It's the law of the universe. Trust me. So go out there and get happy!

"Every happening, great and small, is a parable whereby God speaks to us, and the art of life is to get the message."
~ Malcolm Muggeridge

Acknowledgements

- To my remarkable husband who gave me valuable input, took charge of Jared and Cooper (our precocious pooch), ran the errands, cleaned the house and many times treated us to yummy meals so I could use quality and quantity time at the computer.

- To my ever supportive sister, Mike, who was always eager to read my stories, and who enthusiastically encouraged me to get this thing published. And to her distinguished book club that gave me confidence by giving my rough draft a thumbs up.

- To my magnificent parents who were such great examples and who continually provided their love and support.

- To my son, John, for not only being the devoted, loving younger brother, but Jared's priceless and endless example.

- To my daughter-in-law, Kristy, and my grandchildren, Preston and Ben, for being so caring and thoughtful to their brother-in-law and uncle.

- To all those incredibly kind people who accepted, supported, and encouraged Jared along the way, helping him to become the amazing young man he is today.

- To Cooper's and my early morning walking buddy and good friend, Nancy, who devoted her expertise and patience all through the publication process, and who loves Cooper, too.

- And most importantly, to Jared, for being my gift and my teacher, and to whom I can always count on to laugh at my jokes.

If you would like to find a group affiliate in your area, or are interested in knowing more about Down syndrome, or would like to make a contribution to either the National Down Syndrome Congress or your own neighborhood group affiliate, go to **ndsccenter.org.**

Life, Lessons and Laughter can be purchased at Amazon.com or BarnsandNoble.com as either a paperback book or an e-book.

About the Author

Diane Cassity spent the beginning of her career as a physical education instructor and gymnastics coach at a local university. After the birth of her two sons, Jared and John, she gave up that career to begin another: being Mom.

In 1978, she and a good friend, Sally Beal, were not happy with the status quo of available information and the lack of support for parents who had children with Downs, so together they established the Utah Down Syndrome Foundation. It has been helping parents and families ever since.

In 2005 she and her husband collaborated on their first book, a novel, entitled *Target Windridge*. She is currently enjoying retirement in her favorite location, a mountainside, accompanied by her husband Lee, her oldest son Jared, and their current furry family affiliate, Cooper.

(Jared, Lee, Grandpa Whiteley, John, and Diane)

21139900R00153

Made in the USA
San Bernardino, CA
08 January 2019